DARK WHISPERS: The Urban Legend Encyclopedia - Terrifying Tales from Around the World

E.V. Nocturne

Copyright © 2025 by E.V. Nocturne

All rights reserved.

No part of this book may be reproduced in any form or by any electronic or mechanical means, including information storage and retrieval systems, without written permission from the author, except for the use of brief quotations in a book review.

Contents

Introduction: What Makes a Legend? vii

Part 1
America – The Monsters in the Mirror

1. Slender Man (USA) 3
2. Bloody Mary (USA/UK) 7
3. The Rake (Internet-Born) 14
4. The Bell Witch (Tennessee, USA) 20
5. Black-Eyed Children (USA) 25
6. The Bunny Man (Virginia, USA) 31
7. The Legend of Cropsey (New York, USA) 37
   Mini-Feature: "Urban Legends Born from Creepypasta" 43

Part 2
Latin America – Ghosts that Cry and Bite

8. La Llorona (Mexico) 51
9. El Silbón (Venezuela) 57
10. La Planchada (Mexico) 63
11. El Chupacabra (Puerto Rico) 68
12. El Muerto (Texas/Mexico Border) 74
    Mini-Feature: "Day of the Dead and the Blurring of Realms" 79

Part 3
Europe – Haunted Roads and Vengeful Spirits

13. The Vanishing Hitchhiker (UK) 87
14. The White Lady (Germany/Netherlands) 93
15. Krampus (Austria) 99

16. The Green Children of Woolpit (UK)	104
17. Spring-Heeled Jack (Victorian London)	109
Mini-feature: "Medieval Superstitions That Never Died"	115

Part 4
Africa – Shadows, Warnings, and Witches

18. Tokoloshe (South Africa)	123
19. Madam Koi Koi (Nigeria)	129
20. Pinky Pinky (South Africa)	135
21. The Adze (Ghana / Togo)	141
22. The Night Whistler (Kenya)	146
Mini-feature: "Fear and Folklore in Colonial Contexts"	153

Part 5
Asia – Spirits in Mirrors, Games, and Alleys

23. Kuchisake-onna (Japan)	159
24. The Elevator Game (Korea)	165
25. Nale Ba (India)	171
26. Pontianak (Malaysia/Indonesia)	177
27. Jikininki (Japan)	183
28. Mini-feature: "Internet Legends of East Asia: Reddit, LINE, and YouTube"	189

Part 6
Oceania – Lights, Beasts, and Ancient Terrors

29. Min Min Lights (Australia)	197
30. Taniwha (New Zealand/Maori)	203
31. The Dreamtime Beings (Aboriginal Australia)	209
32. The Night Parrot Curse (Outback legend)	215
33. Mini-feature: "The Outback: A Natural Setting for Fear"	221

| CONCLUSION | 227 |
| Appendix | 233 |

Introduction: What Makes a Legend?

Introduction: What Makes a Legend?

You probably shouldn't be reading this alone.

Because by the time you finish this sentence, you'll start to notice the quiet creaks in your house. The shadows at the corner of your vision. The whisper you thought you heard from behind the bathroom mirror. You'll begin to wonder: *Is that just my imagination… or did I bring something back with me from the page?*

We tell ourselves they're *just stories*. We laugh them off around the campfire. We roll our eyes at creepy TikToks or Reddit threads posted at 3 a.m. But deep down, we know better. Urban legends *stick*. They burrow under our skin, slither into our dreams, and sit beside us in the dark. Why? Because they sound like they could be true—and sometimes, they are.

Introduction: What Makes a Legend?

The Anatomy of a Legend

Urban legends aren't ancient myths passed down by tribal elders or found carved into ancient stone. They're something *closer. Newer. Deadlier.* These stories live in whispers, in text messages, in strange YouTube videos that vanish an hour after you see them.

Whereas traditional folklore tells of gods, monsters, and moral fables, **urban legends** deal in the here and now:

- A vanishing hitchhiker on a road near your town.
- A game that promises to summon a spirit if you dare to play it.
- A girl who appears in mirrors if you say her name three times.
- A friend of a friend who saw something they were *never meant to see.*

They're told as true. They travel fast. They evolve in real time.

From Campfires to Creepypastas

Before the internet, legends spread through word of mouth—passed between kids at sleepovers, whispered in the halls at school, scribbled into the margins of diaries. But then came the forums. Then came creepypasta. Then came TikTok.

Suddenly, the shadows had usernames.

In the last twenty years, the way we experience horror has changed. Urban legends now come with proof—blurry photos, fake news clippings, first-person testimonies. Slender Man was born on a Photoshop thread. Smile Dog came with an

Introduction: What Makes a Legend?

image you were warned *never* to look at. The Elevator Game spread like a ritual through YouTube, said to transport you to another dimension.

These aren't stories you find in dusty books—they find *you*, in the feed, in the algorithm, at night.

Why We Keep Telling Them

So what gives these stories their staying power?

Urban legends are sticky because they scare us in ways we *recognize*. They reflect our modern fears:

- Fear of being watched

- Fear of the unknown

- Fear of losing control

- Fear that *maybe... there's more to this world than we admit*

They comfort us by offering explanations for the unexplainable. They thrill us by turning the mundane into the terrifying. And they keep us connected—generationally, globally, even virally.

Most of all? They make fear fun. Controlled. Safe. Until it isn't.

How This Book Works

Dark Whispers is your passport to the creepiest corners of the planet—one story at a time. Inside, you'll find terrifying tales divided by region, each legend brought to life with:

- A narrative retelling

- Its cultural origin and meaning

Introduction: What Makes a Legend?

- How it spread (from folklore to forums)
- A "Scare Rating" and a "Truth Meter"
- Modern versions seen in creepypasta, TikTok, and urban life

You'll also find mini-interludes filled with creepy testimonies, internet rabbit holes, and real accounts that blur the line between fiction and fact. At the end of the book, you'll even have a toolkit to help you craft your own legend—if you dare.

A Final Warning

These stories are more than entertainment. They have power. Power given to them by those who believe... and by those who listen.

So as you read, keep something in mind:

Some say that simply *knowing* a legend is enough to bring it closer.

To awaken it.

To *invite it in*.

Sleep tight.

Part 1

America – The Monsters in the Mirror

They lurk in the woods. They wait behind the glass. They smile when no one else is watching.

Chapter 1
Slender Man (USA)

"He has no face, no name, and no mercy"

You never *see* him at first.

Only the feeling—cold breath against your neck, the weight of invisible eyes watching from the woods.

You tell yourself it's nothing. A trick of the wind. A shadow cast by trees.

But then your phone glitches. Static buzzes through your earbuds. And in the photos you just took... there he is.

Tall. Faceless. Waiting.

The first time Slender Man appeared, it was on an internet forum.

A photoshopped image. A grainy black-and-white picture of children playing near the trees, with something wrong in the background.

Something tall. Something wearing a suit. Something no one else noticed.

Until it was too late.

He wasn't real. Not at first. Just a spooky image, a little text, a caption that hinted at something ancient and evil.

But legends don't need birth certificates. They only need belief.

Soon, he was everywhere.

In fan art, web series, whispered bedtime warnings.

He slithered into horror games, YouTube rabbit holes, middle school sleepovers.

No one could agree on what he was—but everyone agreed on what he did:

He took children.

You can't run from someone who doesn't move.

You can't fight something that doesn't speak.

And you can't forget a face that doesn't exist.

They say he causes nightmares. Hallucinations. Madness.

They say if you see him once, you'll see him again.

And again.

And again.

Until you don't wake up at all.

Then came **the stabbing**.

Two 12-year-old girls. A forest in Wisconsin.

Nineteen wounds carved into a friend's body—all to prove their loyalty to a creature that didn't exist.

Or maybe one that had been summoned by belief alone.

The world gasped. Parents panicked.

And suddenly, Slender Man wasn't just an internet story. He was a threat. A cautionary tale. A scapegoat.

The monster had *left* the screen.

But legends don't die. They adapt.

He haunts TikToks now. Creeps through hashtags. Appears in grainy backwoods dash cam footage.

He's changed names. Shifted forms.

But he's still watching.

From behind the trees.

From the edge of your frame.

From the silence.

E.V. Nocturne

He doesn't speak. He doesn't move.

He just waits—patient, hungry, blank.

Scare Rating: 💀 💀 💀 💀
Truth Meter: 💀 Pure fiction... except when it isn't.
First Sighting: June 10, 2009
Known For: Being the first viral horror myth of the internet age
Where He Lurks Now: Games (*Slender: The Eight Pages*), YouTube (*Marble Hornets*), TikTok, dreams

You don't need to summon him.

You only need to know his name.

And now... you do.

Chapter 2
Bloody Mary (USA/UK)

"Say her name three times—and pray she doesn't answer."

You know the ritual.

Turn off the lights.

Stand in front of the mirror.

Say her name: **Bloody Mary. Bloody Mary. Bloody Mary.**

And wait.

Some say she'll appear instantly—her face twisted, bleeding, mouth wide with a scream.

Some say she'll reach through the glass.

Some say you'll see your own death reflected back at you.

And some say… nothing happens.

Until later.

. . .

No one knows exactly where she came from.

But everyone has a version of her.

She's the ghost of a vengeful woman.

Or a wrongly accused witch.

Or a murdered child seeking justice.

Or maybe... just a game gone wrong that no one dares finish.

Legends warp like smoke. And mirrors? They lie.

Reflections in the Dark

You heard the story from your cousin.

They heard it from a classmate.

Who heard it from an older sibling who swears—swears—it really happened.

She tried it at a sleepover.

In the middle of the night.

Lit a candle. Faced the mirror. Spoke the name.

And screamed.

They say she saw something in the glass that never went away.

The earliest whispers of Bloody Mary go back **centuries**.

Some connect her to **Queen Mary I of England**—nicknamed "Bloody Mary" for burning Protestants at the stake.

Others say she was a midwife who killed newborns, or a woman who lost her baby and still searches for it… in the faces of those who summon her.

In every version, she's tied to:

- **Blood**
- **Mirrors**
- **Vengeance**

And above all, **a name that should not be spoken aloud**.

The Ritual

There are many ways to summon her.

Every region has its rules. Every friend adds a new twist.

The most common version goes like this:

1 Go into a bathroom with no windows.

2 Turn off the lights.

3 Light a single candle.

4 Stand in front of the mirror.

5 Say her name three times.

6 Don't blink.

And if you do it right...

She comes.

Sometimes she appears behind you.

Sometimes she replaces your reflection.

Sometimes you vanish—and your friends only find blood and a shattered mirror.

No one ever tells the *full* story.

Because the ones who saw her? They don't talk about it.

The Psychology of a Curse

Why is **Bloody Mary** so powerful?

Because she lives in the **space between fear and fascination**.

We know she's not real... but what if she is?

The mirror is a symbol of identity—and distortion.

In psychology, staring at your own face in low light can cause illusions, even hallucinations.

Combine that with superstition, darkness, and peer pressure, and you have the perfect setting for **urban ritual**.

She's a **test**:

- Of bravery.

- Of belief.

- Of how far we'll go just to say we did it.

. . .

Global Variants and Sister Spirits

Bloody Mary doesn't haunt the world alone.

- **Japan** has *Hanako-san*, a ghost girl who haunts school bathrooms.

- **Mexico** has *La Llorona*, the weeping woman who searches for her drowned children.

- **Russia** has *The Queen of Spades*, who is summoned through mirror games.

- Even ancient Rome feared "mirror spirits" that could be trapped behind glass.

The theme is universal: **female rage, grief, and ghostliness**, trapped in reflection.

From Schoolyards to Screens

Bloody Mary has become a rite of passage for schoolchildren —and a source of **endless retellings** online.

- **YouTube challenges**: Thousands of videos of teens daring each other to summon her.

- **Creepypasta stories**: Each more gruesome than the last.

- **TikTok rituals**: Users claim they "saw something" they can't explain.

- **Movies**: Including *Urban Legend*, *Paranormal Activity 3*, *Bloody Mary (2005)*—each reinterpreting her myth.

She shifts shape across platforms but always keeps her core:

Face the mirror. Face yourself. And maybe... face her.

Why She Endures

Because the mirror is *too tempting*.

Because we want to know what's on the other side.

Because we *need* to believe we're brave enough to look.

And maybe, just maybe, she's real—**because we keep making her real.**

We speak her name.

We pass her story.

We test the glass.

And when the lights go out, we all wonder... *what if I tried it?*

- **Scare Rating:** 💀 💀 💀 💀 💀
- **Truth Meter:** 🧬 Folklore-inspired, amplified by fear
- **Earliest Known Origin:** 1970s American sleepover lore (possibly older)
- **Possible Inspiration:** Queen Mary I, witch trials, mirror phobia
- **Modern Appearances:** TikTok rituals, creepypastas, teen horror films

Final Words

You're probably tempted to try it now.

To go into your bathroom. Turn off the lights. Say the words.

Just to see.

But don't.

Mirrors remember.

And some names are doors.

Chapter 3
The Rake (Internet-Born)

"It waits at the foot of your bed—and it never blinks."

They say it crouches there, inches from your face, while you sleep.

Not breathing.

Not blinking.

Just **watching**.

And if you wake up too soon… it doesn't run.

It smiles.

The Rake isn't something ancient.

It doesn't come from dusty libraries or centuries-old folklore.

It comes from *here*—the internet.

A creation born in forums, nurtured by fear, and raised in shadows.

But that doesn't make it any less dangerous.

In fact, it makes it worse.

Because it doesn't *need* a graveyard. It only needs a screen.

The Origin of the Rake

In 2005, a post appeared online.

An invitation: *Let's create a new monster.*

Users responded with journal entries, eyewitness accounts, and survivor testimony—all describing the same thing:

"I woke up in the middle of the night... and saw it sitting at the foot of my bed. Pale. Hairless. Its eyes were black and empty, and it just... stared."

A creature that crept into homes.

That whispered while you slept.

That sometimes left you alone—and sometimes left you in pieces.

It was dubbed **The Rake**—a name with no known origin, but one that felt *wrong* in your mouth. Like something sharp.

It spread like wildfire.

Copied. Shared. Believed.

· · ·

What Is the Rake?

Descriptions vary, but the **core traits** remain the same:

- Emaciated, humanoid body
- Long fingers and claws like bone sickles
- Pale, smooth, almost wet-looking skin
- Hollow, sunken eyes—or none at all
- Moves on all fours, like a twisted dog or spider

It's always **naked**, but not vulnerable.

Always silent, but never still for long.

And it watches. **Always watches.**

Some say it speaks—but only in whispers, and only to those already marked.

The Rake's Modus Operandi

- Appears **at night**, usually in the subject's home
- Sits at the edge of the bed, staring, waiting
- Victims report waking with intense fear, dread, or sleep paralysis
- Leaves scratch marks—or **takes something** that can't be described
- In some stories: it disappears when seen

In others: *that's when it attacks*

Sometimes it does nothing. Just watches.

And somehow... that's worse.

Sleep Paralysis, Explained?

Many believe the Rake is a **modern embodiment of sleep paralysis demons**:

- Old folklore had "The Old Hag" sitting on your chest
- Night terrors included hallucinations of dark figures, evil watchers
- Now, in the age of viral horror, we have the Rake

He's not just under the bed—he's the fear *of not being able to scream.*

Why It Works: Minimalism as Fear

What makes the Rake terrifying isn't gore or detail—it's **implication**.

He's not tied to any one story.

He has no clear motive.

No explanation.

No origin.

He just **is**.

Like a bad thought. Like guilt. Like a disease.

He leaves behind scars—physical, emotional, psychic—and then disappears into digital static.

He's fear, stripped to the bone.

Pop Culture & Modern Haunts

Though less "mainstream" than Slender Man, the Rake remains a cult icon in digital horror.

• **YouTube sightings**: Found-footage shorts show him lurking in woods, under beds, or crawling across highways

• **Gaming appearances**: Mods and indie horror titles include him as a roaming stalker or jumpscare entity

• **TikTok**: Quick flashes, shadow creature edits, scream reactions tagged #therake

• **Fan fiction & Reddit**: "Survivor accounts," sleep logs, and supposed security cam footage

He's not a mascot. He's a **lurker**.

He never becomes a meme—because he's too quiet for that.

- **Scare Rating:** 💀 💀 💀 💀
- **Truth Meter:** 🌐 Internet-born but psychologically real
- **Known For:** Sleep paralysis themes, silence, subtle horror
- **Creepypasta Debut:** Circa 2005–2006, developed through collaborative writing
- **Similar To:** The Smiling Man, The Watcher, The Shadow People

. . .

Final Words

The Rake has no legend to protect it.

No name in old books. No worshippers. No curses.

That's what makes it worse.

It doesn't **need** your belief to exist.

Just your attention.

Just your fear.

And now that you've read this?

He knows where you sleep.

Chapter 4
The Bell Witch (Tennessee, USA)

"She spoke, slapped, and screamed in the dark—and she never left."

Some hauntings whisper.

This one **spoke.**

It shouted. It slapped. It sang hymns in a voice no one recognized and **laughed** when they prayed.

They called her the **Bell Witch.**

And in the quiet Tennessee countryside, the Bell family learned that *not all ghosts are shy.*

Some want you to hear them scream.

It began with scratching.

Under the floorboards. Behind the walls. In the corners of the children's rooms.

Then came the **tapping**.

Then **the voice**.

And once it started, it didn't stop.

The Bell Family Haunting (1817–1821)

In a remote farmhouse in Adams, Tennessee, farmer **John Bell** and his family lived a quiet life—until they didn't.

First, it was strange animals in the fields.

Then, the children complained of being pinched in their sleep.

John saw a creature with a rabbit's head and a dog's body staring at him from the edge of the woods.

Then the **entity spoke**.

And suddenly, the Bell family wasn't living alone anymore.

The Witch with a Voice

Unlike other ghosts of the time, this one **spoke freely**.

It recited sermons word-for-word from miles away.

It mimicked the voices of family members.

It answered questions—sometimes truthfully, sometimes **cruelly**.

And it made clear its hatred for one man in particular: **John Bell.**

It cursed him. Followed him.

And in 1820, John Bell mysteriously died—after years of torment.

The entity took credit.

"I fixed him."

Violent, Vocal, and Vengeful

The Bell Witch didn't just haunt.

She **assaulted**.

She slapped the children. Pulled their hair.

Choked John Bell's daughter Betsy in her sleep.

Mocked guests. Swore in multiple languages.

No priest could banish her.

No wall could stop her.

She was everywhere—and she seemed to enjoy the fear.

Was It a Spirit, or Something Worse?

Locals believed it was a **witch**, the ghost of **Kate Batts**, a woman rumored to have cursed the Bells over a land dispute.

Others said it was a **poltergeist**—a restless energy attached to emotion.

Some even claimed it wasn't a ghost at all, but something **older**, something *that speaks through spirits*—a mimic, a demon, a trickster wearing the face of the dead.

What makes the Bell Witch story different is how **public** it became.

Visitors, neighbors, even soldiers were said to have heard her voice.

This wasn't a private terror. This was **a performance**.

Historical Notes & Real Records

- The haunting was written about in *"An Authenticated History of the Bell Witch"* by Martin Van Buren Ingram in 1894

- President **Andrew Jackson** allegedly visited the Bell property and said:

"I'd rather fight the British again than deal with that witch."

- The **Bell Witch Cave**, near the original farm site, is still a tourist attraction—said to remain **active**

Why She Still Haunts Us

The Bell Witch story endures because it's not subtle.

She wasn't fleeting shadows or cold spots. She was **loud, vocal, physical.**

She **spoke your name**.

She **knew your secrets**.

She **never shut up**.

Most ghosts are passive. The Bell Witch was **in control**.

And worse—she wanted an audience.

She was *the first American celebrity ghost*.

- **Scare Rating:** 💀 💀 💀 💀
- **Truth Meter:** Based on 19th-century written accounts, partially verifiable
- **Location:** Adams, Tennessee
- **Key Victims:** John Bell, Betsy Bell
- **Modern Tie-Ins:** Ghost tours, documentaries, horror film *An American Haunting* (2005)

Final Words

Some ghosts fade. Some get bored. Some move on.

Not this one.

The Bell Witch didn't just haunt a house—she haunted a *legacy*.

And if you listen closely enough, they say you can still hear her.

Laughing.

Whispering.

Waiting.

Chapter 5
Black-Eyed Children (USA)

"They knock. They ask to come in. Whatever you do—don't say yes."

It starts with a knock.

You check the time—too late for visitors.

But it's not a delivery. Not the neighbors. Not anyone you know.

You peek through the window.

There are two kids on your porch.

A boy and a girl. Or maybe two boys. Dressed oddly. Standing too still.

They're not looking at you.

They're looking **through** you.

Then they speak.

"Can we come in? We need help. Please. We're cold."

You almost open the door.

Until you see their eyes.

Black. No whites. No pupils. Just void.

The First Encounter

The legend began in **1996**, with a post by journalist **Brian Bethel**.

He described stopping at a strip mall in Abilene, Texas, to write a check.

Two boys knocked on his car window. Said they wanted a ride home.

They weren't threatening. They were calm. Too calm.

He felt **irrational fear**, like his body knew something his mind didn't.

Then he noticed their eyes—**entirely black**.

No irises. No color. Just endless dark.

When he hesitated, their voices changed.

Their tone dropped.

"We can't come in unless you invite us."

He drove away, heart pounding, feeling as though he'd just escaped something ancient.

. . .

Who—or What—Are They?

Descriptions vary, but all reports share disturbing commonalities:

- Children aged 6 to 16
- Pale or grayish skin
- Obsolete or "off" clothing (like from another era)
- Dull or robotic speech
- And of course... **jet-black eyes**

They speak with politeness—but with **urgency**, always asking to be let in:

- Into your car
- Your house
- Your hotel room
- Anywhere that feels *safe*

But once you look into their eyes, you don't feel safe at all.

Vampires? Demons? Aliens?

No one knows what they are.

Some say they're **vampiric entities**—requiring an invitation to enter.

Others think they're **demonic tricksters**, using innocence as a mask.

Some believe they're **extraterrestrials**, experimenting with human fear.

Whatever the theory, everyone agrees:

Letting them in means something *bad* happens.

There are stories—unconfirmed—of those who did invite them in.

They never say what happened next.

They just disappear from the story.

The Psychology of the Uncanny Child

Why are they so terrifying?

Because they **almost** seem human.

But not quite.

There's a name for it: the **uncanny valley**—the discomfort we feel when something is *too close* to real, but just *wrong enough* to unsettle us.

We're wired to protect children.

So when a child becomes the **threat**, our brains recoil in horror.

Especially when they ask so **calmly** to be let in.

Modern Sightings & Digital Lore

Black-Eyed Children have become digital folklore icons:

- **Reddit horror threads** with new encounters posted regularly

- **YouTube reenactments** and "caught on camera" videos

- **Creepypasta retellings**, each adding chilling variations

- **TikTok POV videos** with eerie knocking and voiceovers

- Referenced in shows like *Monsters and Mysteries in America*, *Paranormal Witness*, and podcasts like *Lore*

They're modern boogeymen, updated for the internet age—tied to no specific place, no culture, no time.

They could appear **anywhere**.

Even your doorstep.

- **Scare Rating:** 💀 💀 💀 💀 💀
- **Truth Meter:** Modern folklore with viral roots
- **First Known Report:** 1996 (Brian Bethel, Texas)
- **Common Settings:** Cars, porches, hotels, roadside stops
- **Catchphrases:**
  - "We need to use your phone."
  - "We're lost."
  - "Can we come in?"

Final Words

If you hear a knock late at night—

If the children outside are too still, too quiet, too calm—

If their voices make your stomach twist and your lights flicker—

Don't open the door.

They can't come in without permission.

But once you say yes...

You'll never get them out.

Chapter 6
The Bunny Man (Virginia, USA)

"He wore a white suit. He carried an axe. And he hated trespassers."

They thought it was a Halloween prank.

A man in a bunny costume. Standing under a bridge. Holding something in his hand.

Until he threw it.

An axe—whirling through the air, slamming into the side of their car.

They didn't stop to ask questions.

They just drove. Fast.

The Bridge Where It Began

It was **1970**, in **Fairfax County, Virginia**.

Two incidents. Two witnesses. Both describing the same thing:

- A man dressed in a white bunny suit

- Lurking near a rural overpass now known as **Bunny Man Bridge**

- Armed with a hatchet or axe

- Angry. Silent. Watching.

The first couple said he screamed at them for trespassing before hurling an axe at their windshield.

The second report—only days later—came from a security guard who saw a man hacking at a porch railing, still wearing the costume, before vanishing into the woods.

Police searched. Local papers ran the story.

And just like that—a **legend was born**.

Fact, Fiction, and Fur

No one was ever caught.

No one ever confessed.

But the **Bunny Man** didn't need to be real to become *real*.

Stories spread like wildfire through Fairfax County:

- A lunatic escaped from an asylum

- He lived in the woods, dressed as a rabbit

- He slaughtered teenagers who snuck into the area at night
- Sometimes he hung their bodies from the bridge—*by their feet*

Of course, there was **no asylum nearby**.

No missing records. No confirmed murders.

Just whispers. Just fear.

But that's all a legend ever needs.

Why a Bunny?

The question that haunts every retelling:

Why the suit?

Some say it was to mock childhood innocence.

Others say it was meant to hide his identity.

One theory suggests he thought he *was* the rabbit—an unhinged mind wearing the symbol of what it believed it had become.

But maybe the scariest possibility?

He was just *a guy in a bunny costume with an axe.*

And that's all it takes.

The Urban Ritual

Today, **Bunny Man Bridge** is a pilgrimage site for horror fans.

On Halloween, thrill-seekers gather at the overpass—hoping to see something, hear something, **summon** something.

They tell the story, then wait.

Some say they hear scratching from under the bridge.

Some say they find small tufts of white fur.

Some say they saw *him*, standing just beyond the trees.

The police regularly clear people out—but the legend grows stronger every year.

The Bunny Man in Pop Culture

• Referenced in horror films like *Donnie Darko*, *Bunnyman*, and *The Strangers: Prey at Night*

• Appears in video games, indie slasher shorts, and creepypasta spinoffs

• Inspires countless *YouTube exploration videos* of the bridge at night

• Urban legend podcasts (like *Astonishing Legends* and *Lore*) have devoted episodes to his tale

He's a **cult icon**—equal parts slasher, trickster, and nightmare Easter Bunny.

Why It Works

The Bunny Man works because it's *absurd*—and that makes it **unpredictable**.

We expect ghosts in graveyards.

We expect monsters in the dark.

We don't expect a man in a bunny suit with an axe.

That *disconnect* is what gets under your skin.

He doesn't fit the rules.

He doesn't follow a pattern.

And if he's still out there—he could be *anywhere*.

- **Scare Rating:** 💀 💀 💀
- **Truth Meter:** 🪦 Based on real police reports, spun into folklore
- **First Report:** October 1970, Fairfax County, Virginia
- **Common Location:** Colchester Overpass ("Bunny Man Bridge")
- **Sightings Still Reported:** Almost every Halloween

Final Words

You're driving down a back road. The woods are too quiet.

Up ahead is a bridge. Just a bridge. Nothing special.

E.V. Nocturne

You slow down.

And then you see him.

A man in white. Staring from the trees.

Not running. Not hiding.

Just waiting.

With an axe in his hand.

Chapter 7
The Legend of Cropsey (New York, USA)

"Every town has a child-snatcher story. This one just might be real."

He was the monster kids whispered about at sleepaway camp.

The escaped mental patient who lived in the woods.

The one with a hook for a hand, or a rusty axe, or a bag full of bones.

He only came out at night.

He only took **bad children**.

They called him **Cropsey**.

And for decades, New York kids feared him.

They didn't know they should've been afraid of **something much worse**.

• • •

Born in the Shadows of Staten Island

In the 1970s and '80s, every child in Staten Island knew about Cropsey.

He lived in the **abandoned ruins of the Willowbrook State School**—a decaying institution that once held hundreds of children with disabilities, many of them neglected or abused.

Campers said he was a janitor who went mad after the school closed.

Some said he lost his own child and now hunted others.

Others swore they saw him near the woods at night, dragging a sack through the leaves.

It was the perfect urban legend:

- A real place

- A real history

- And a warning: **Don't wander too far. Cropsey will get you.**

Then the Children Started Disappearing

Between 1972 and 1987, **five children** vanished from Staten Island.

- Jennifer Schweiger, a 12-year-old girl with Down syndrome, was the one they found—buried in a shallow grave near the abandoned Willowbrook School.

- The other children were never seen again.

The prime suspect?

A homeless man named **Andre Rand**—a former orderly at Willowbrook.

He was arrested. Charged. Convicted.

And suddenly, the **legend had a face.**

Andre Rand: The Man Behind the Myth

Rand was no ghost story.

He was real.

And his past was **terrifying**.

- Former mental health employee
- Arrested multiple times for kidnapping, attempted sexual assault, and suspicious behavior around schools
- Lived in the woods, often in makeshift shelters and tunnels near the Willowbrook site

Though only convicted in Jennifer's case, Rand is **suspected in multiple disappearances.**

He became **Cropsey**, redefined—flesh and blood born from myth and fear.

The Documentary That Changed Everything

In 2009, the film *Cropsey* debuted at Tribeca Film Festival.

It was created by two Staten Island natives who grew up fearing the legend—and uncovered its shocking truth.

The documentary:

- Traced the evolution of the Cropsey myth
- Investigated the real-life disappearances
- Revealed how urban legends and true crime can **merge**

It ended with a haunting question:

Was the legend made real by fear—or was fear just trying to explain something real?

Willowbrook: The Heart of Horror

The Willowbrook State School wasn't just background noise—it was horror incarnate.

Closed in the 1980s after a **massive abuse scandal**, the school was exposed in a famous segment by **Geraldo Rivera**.

Children left naked, unfed, restrained, crawling in filth.

Some say Cropsey is a ghost born of their pain.

Others say Willowbrook **created monsters**, both imagined and real.

To this day, people explore the site.

And many say it still feels… wrong.

. . .

Why Cropsey Haunts So Deeply

Most urban legends stay fiction.

Cropsey didn't.

He blurs the lines:

- A **warning tale** that mirrored **real danger**
- A **monster myth** that matched **a predator**
- A **ghost story** born from **systemic horror**

Cropsey became more than a name.

He became a **symbol** of the fears adults ignored.

- • **Scare Rating:** 💀 💀 💀 💀 💀
- • **Truth Meter:** ⚖️ Urban legend built on true crime
- • **Real Site:** Willowbrook State School, Staten Island, NY
- • **Key Case:** Jennifer Schweiger (1987)
- • **Must-Watch:** *Cropsey* documentary (2009)

Final Words

The scariest legends are the ones that don't end when the story stops.

They leave footprints.

They leave victims.

E.V. Nocturne

They leave questions no one wants answered.

Cropsey might not be one man anymore.

He might be every missing child case with no closure.

Every place we pretend isn't haunted.

Every face we forget—until it comes back.

Mini-Feature: "Urban Legends Born from Creepypasta"

"Once upon a time... on the internet."

Not all legends are old.

Some were born yesterday.

Some were born on forums, stitched together in Reddit threads, built from grainy images, midnight posts, and the electric hum of fear shared through screens.

They are **creepypastas**—a portmanteau of "copy-paste"—digital horror stories copied, shared, remixed, and believed.

In the right hands, they become **modern myths**.

And some have grown too big to stay on the screen.

1. Jeff the Killer

"Go to sleep."

His smile is cut too wide.

Mini-Feature: "Urban Legends Born from Creepypasta"

His eyelids are burned off.

He stares while you sleep, then whispers those three words before plunging the knife.

Jeff the Killer started as an image—a grotesque face, pale as death, with shadowed eyes and a smeared, eternal grin.

The story followed: a boy named Jeff who was bullied, disfigured, and driven to madness. Now, he lurks in the dark, waiting to make others *just like him.*

He's become one of the most recognized creepypasta figures—despite, or because of, how disturbing his origin image is.

2. Smile Dog

"Spread the word."

A cursed image file—**smile.jpg**.

It shows a dog... but not a real one.

Its grin is impossibly wide. Its eyes are human. Its presence is **wrong.**

Everyone who opens the file begins to suffer nightmares, hallucinations, and suicidal thoughts. They hear whispering voices. See the dog in their dreams.

The only way to stop it?

Send the image to someone else.

Smile Dog is a **digital chain letter** from hell.

And you never forget his face.

Mini-Feature: "Urban Legends Born from Creepypasta"

3. The Expressionless

"She wasn't breathing. But she was smiling."

In a hospital in 1972, a woman walks in wearing a white gown—covered in blood.

She doesn't speak. She doesn't blink. Her face is... **wrong**. Plastic. Frozen in a blank, eerie smile.

She tears through the staff, killing several before whispering:

"I am... God."

Though the story is fake (and widely debunked), its **haunting photo**—a mannequin with dead eyes and red lips—continues to circulate.

People still ask if it really happened.

That's the power of creepypasta.

4. Zalgo

"He comes."

Zalgo isn't a creature. He's a **concept**.

A corruption. A glitch in the code of reality.

When Zalgo arrives, text becomes corrupted. Images melt. Logic bends.

He's often mentioned when things "break":

- Characters in comics speak in gibberish.
- Fonts dissolve into chaos.
- Cartoons turn violent without warning.

Mini-Feature: "Urban Legends Born from Creepypasta"

Zalgo represents **internet madness**—a digital Lovecraftian god that consumes narratives and warps everything around it.

You don't summon Zalgo.

You just notice him too late.

Why These Legends Matter

Creepypasta gave rise to a **new era of folklore**—built not from oral storytelling, but **shared content**.

And just like old legends, they:

• Reflect our fears (technology, isolation, loss of control)

• Invite participation (remixes, roleplays, ARGs)

• Spread through belief and repetition

They live not in woods or mirrors—but in forums, file folders, and forgotten links.

- **Jeff the Killer:** Psychotic teen turned supernatural killer.
  Scare Rating: 💀 💀 💀
- **Smile Dog:** Cursed image file that drives viewers mad.
  Scare Rating: 💀 💀 💀 💀
- **The Expressionless:** Hospital horror with viral photo.
  Scare Rating: 💀 💀
- **Zalgo:** Digital chaos being; corrupts media and minds.
  Scare Rating: 💀 💀 💀 💀

Final Thought

The campfire is gone.

Now we gather around glowing screens.

We don't pass stories in whispers—we post them. Tag them. Watch them go viral.

But the fear?

That part hasn't changed.

Part 2

Latin America – Ghosts that Cry and Bite

In these stories, death doesn't rest. It weeps, it wanders, it hungers.

Chapter 8
La Llorona (Mexico)

"She weeps for the children she drowned. And if she sees yours... she might take them too."

You hear her before you see her.

A cry—sharp, distant, but getting closer.

The sound of a woman weeping.

Calling out in the dark.

"¡Ay, mis hijos!"

"Oh, my children!"

You tell yourself it's just wind.

Or an animal. Or maybe the river moving funny.

But you don't move.

Because something in you knows: **that voice isn't human anymore.**

She is **La Llorona**—*The Weeping Woman*.

And if you hear her cry... it might already be too late.

A Mother's Curse

No one agrees on the full story.

But everyone agrees on how it ends.

A woman. Beautiful, proud, and poor.

Some say her name was Maria.

She falls in love with a rich man—a soldier, a noble, a stranger passing through town. He gives her children, promises, dreams.

But one day, he leaves.

Or worse—he returns... with a **new wife**.

Maria breaks.

In a moment of grief, or fury, or both, she takes her two children to the river.

And drowns them.

When she realizes what she's done, she wails.

She wails until her voice splits the sky.

Then she drowns herself.

. . .

But the river doesn't accept her.

Instead, she is cursed to walk the earth, her soul **torn between sorrow and rage**.

She searches endlessly for her lost children.

And when she can't find them...

She takes yours.

What the Legend Says

La Llorona is usually seen near rivers, creeks, and bridges—especially at night.

She wears a long, white dress.

Sometimes soaked and stained.

Sometimes glowing like moonlight.

Her hair is black and wild.

Her face is hidden—or twisted with grief.

And her cry?

It cuts through you.

Not just because it's sad.

But because **something inside you recognizes it**.

Children who hear her may go missing.

She lures them with sweetness... or screams.

Adults who mock her or follow her cry have been known to vanish or go mad.

In some versions, if you hear her from far away—she's near.

And if she sounds close... she's not.

She floats. She watches. She waits.

Fear as a Teaching Tool

La Llorona is more than a ghost. She's a **warning**.

- Don't play near the river at night.
- Don't stay out too late.
- Don't disobey your parents.

Generations of Latinx children have been raised with her voice echoing in their heads.

But she's also more than fear.

She is **grief**.

She is **guilt**.

She is the **shadow of womanhood twisted by betrayal**.

She's Everywhere

Though born in Mexico, La Llorona's wail has spread:

- Through Latin America under different names (La Malora, La Lamentadora)

- Into the American Southwest where Mexican and Chicano families still whisper her tale

- Onto TikTok, YouTube, and Reddit—users sharing "recordings" and alleged sightings

She appears in:

- *Coco* (as a playful nod)

- *The Curse of La Llorona* (as a full-blown horror villain)

- Countless songs, poems, street art, and tattoos

She is **cultural memory**. Alive, evolving, unstoppable.

Did She Come from the Conquest?

Some scholars believe La Llorona's roots run deeper than legend.

- **Aztec myth** tells of a goddess named **Cihuacóatl** who mourned her lost children and warned of coming destruction.

- Her cries were said to be heard just before the **Spanish conquest**.

Could La Llorona be the mother of a stolen people?

A spirit mourning not just two children, but **a lost world**?

Her legend may be older than Spain itself.

And more bitter.

- **Scare Rating:** 💀 💀 💀 💀 💀
- **Truth Meter:** 💀 Folkloric, with ancient and colonial layers
- **Known Locations:** Mexico City, Guanajuato, Texas, New Mexico
- **Signature Phrase:** "¡Ay, mis hijos!"
- **Modern Mediums:** TikTok audio trends, horror films, bedtime threats

Final Words

If you ever hear her cry—don't go toward it.

Don't listen. Don't answer.

And don't run, either.

Just stay very, very quiet.

Because once you hear her voice...

she's already seen you.

Chapter 9
El Silbón (Venezuela)

"If you hear his whistle close—run. If it sounds far away... it's already too late."

There's something in the wind.

A whistle. Off-key. Uneven. Floating through the tall grass.

It rises, falls, circles your ears.

And something inside you tightens—your skin, your breath, your blood.

Whoever hears the whistle dies.

That's what they say in the Llanos.

The Boy Who Killed His Father

Once, there was a boy.

Some say he was spoiled. Some say he was just hungry. Some say he was always wicked.

One day, he demanded deer meat from his father.

When his father didn't bring it, the boy—furious—**murdered him**.

He ripped out the man's heart. Brought it to his mother to cook.

She screamed when she learned the truth.

And his grandfather cursed him.

He tied the boy to a tree.

Whipped him.

Rubbed him with alcohol and chili.

Set dogs on him.

And condemned him to wander the earth forever—**with the bones of his father in a sack**.

Now, the boy is no longer a boy.

He is **El Silbón**—*The Whistler*.

The Sound of Death

El Silbón's whistle is a riddle. A trap.

- If it sounds **close**... you're safe.
- If it sounds **far**... he's already standing behind you.

He moves through the Venezuelan and Colombian plains, especially on misty nights.

He targets drunkards, cheaters, and men who disrespect women.

Some say he empties his sack at night and counts the bones one by one outside his victim's house.

If you hear him counting—and he skips a number?

That's *your* bone he's missing.

How He Appears

El Silbón is a tall, thin figure.

Inhumanly tall. Bone-like. Cloaked in rags.

His face is hidden, his presence cold.

And over his shoulder: a heavy **leather sack** filled with bones —or sometimes **human skulls**.

Dogs whine when he's near.

The wind dies.

And the whistling begins.

No one escapes when they hear it *too late*.

Ghost or Judge?

El Silbón isn't just a ghost. He's a **punisher**.

He doesn't kill without reason.

He seeks out the violent, the cruel, the drunk, the disloyal.

His curse became **a warning** for generations:

- Respect your elders.
- Honor your family.
- Don't drink too much.
- Don't be cruel to women.

He's a spirit shaped by **regret and morality**—like death wearing a conscience.

Where He Walks

El Silbón is known across:

- **Venezuela** (especially the plains of Los Llanos)
- **Colombia**
- Parts of **Ecuador**

The legend is told in song, poetry, and bedtime threats.

Some say he follows his victims across **generations**—if your grandfather wronged someone, he may come for *you*.

Others say he appears just once—to **warn you to change.**

If you don't?

He comes back.

Modern Echoes

- **Short films** and horror adaptations often show him as a slow, stalking figure
- **Creepypasta versions** make him an international "whistler of death"
- TikToks now use the whistle sound as a filter—*and people swear it shows up in real-life videos*
- He's even become a **folk antihero** in some stories—haunting abusive men and sparing the innocent

  - **Scare Rating:** 💀 💀 💀 💀
  - **Truth Meter:** Deep folkloric roots, often used as moral teaching
  - **Origin:** Venezuela (Llanos region)
  - **Key Feature:** Bone sack, signature whistle
  - **Haunting Territory:** Plains, rural towns, broken homes

Final Words

The plains are quiet tonight.

Too quiet.

You hear a whistle. It's distant. Barely there.

You turn in a slow circle, heart pounding.

But there's no one there.

That's the trick.

If the whistle sounds far... he's already close.

Chapter 10
La Planchada (Mexico)

"She walks the hospital halls in perfect white, tending to patients no one else can see."

She appears in silence.

Not like the others.

No screams. No sudden flickers. No dragging chains or blood on the walls.

Just a woman.

In a crisp, white nurse's uniform.

Her shoes make no sound.

Her hands are cold, but gentle.

And she only ever shows herself to the sick and dying.

They say she comes to care for those the living have forgotten.

And when she leaves, the bed is smooth.

The patient is comforted.

And the room smells faintly of antiseptic and roses.

She is called **La Planchada**—*The Ironed Lady.*

The Nurse Who Never Left

There are many stories about who she was.

Some say she was a nurse named **Eulalia**, working in a Mexico City hospital.

Diligent. Polite. Respected.

She fell in love with a doctor who promised her everything.

Then he vanished. Left the city. Married someone else.

Eulalia broke. Her light dimmed.

Some say she **let patients die** out of grief.

Others say she **neglected her duties**, and the guilt consumed her.

One night, she was found dead—her uniform still perfectly pressed.

Her soul never left the hospital.

Now she walks the halls, making up for what she lost.

. . .

What Witnesses Say

Patients on the brink of death often report the same thing:

- A kind woman appeared by their bed.

- She held their hand.

- She told them it would be okay.

- When nurses came in, no one else had been assigned to the room.

- But the sheets were freshly folded.

- The IV had been fixed.

- And the patient—somehow—was stable.

Sometimes it's dismissed as **hallucination**.

Sometimes it's written off as a mix-up.

But those who've seen her **know better**.

She's Not There to Hurt You

La Planchada isn't like other spirits.

She's not vengeful. She doesn't punish.

She **helps**.

But her presence is still haunting.

She's a **reminder**:

- That guilt can outlive the body

- That duty doesn't always end with death

- That the dead still walk among us—not out of hate, but out of **unfinished care**

Where She Walks

La Planchada is mostly seen in:

- Mexico City hospitals

- Guadalajara, Tijuana, and other large urban areas

- Older, colonial-style medical centers with long corridors and quiet wards

She always wears white.

Her hair is tightly pulled back.

Her shoes never scuff.

And her uniform? **Flawless. Pressed. Ironed.**

That's how you know it's her.

The Psychology of the Healing Haunt

Ghosts usually follow trauma, not tenderness.

But La Planchada teaches us that **some pain takes the form of kindness.**

That grief doesn't always burn—it can **soften**, too.

It can serve. It can heal.

She is the **opposite of neglect**.

She is **compassion turned into haunting**.

And she makes you wonder:

What if the next nurse who walks through that door... isn't alive?

- **Scare Rating:** 💀💀 (mild, but deeply unsettling)
- **Truth Meter:** 👻 Strongly folkloric, widely told in hospitals
- **Known Locations:** Mexico City, Guadalajara, Monterrey
- **Typical Signs:** Pressed sheets, cold hands, white uniform
- **Other Interpretations:** Guilt spirit, ghost of the overworked, modern La Llorona

Final Words

When the halls go quiet at night...

When the lights dim in the ICU...

When the nurses change shifts and the ward empties—

She appears.

Not to haunt you.

But to help.

Because some promises are so deep... **they follow you past death.**

Chapter 11
El Chupacabra (Puerto Rico)

"It drinks blood. Leaves no tracks. And when it strikes—there's nothing left but dry corpses and fear."

It starts with a scream from the barn.

By the time you run outside, it's too late.

The animals are dead—goats, chickens, maybe even a dog.

But it's not a normal attack.

There's no blood.

No mess.

Just tiny puncture wounds on the neck... and bodies dry as dust.

Something drained them.

Clean. Quiet. Perfect.

Someone whispers the name: **El Chupacabra.**

And no one sleeps that night.

The First Sightings

It began in **Puerto Rico**, in the summer of **1995**.

Farmers reported something strange—livestock killed without any signs of a struggle.

No blood. No bite marks. Just... **emptiness**.

The animals looked vacuumed out from the inside.

Then came eyewitnesses.

A woman described a creature standing on two legs, with:

- Large, glowing red eyes
- Spikes down its back
- Clawed hands
- And a mouth full of fangs

The name came quickly: **Chupacabra**, the "goat sucker."

🗿 What Is It?

Descriptions vary wildly, but here are the two most common versions:

The Reptilian Variant **(Puerto Rico, Central America)**

- Greenish-gray skin

- Spines or quills

- Stands upright

- Looks like a cross between a reptile and an alien

The Canine Variant (Texas, Mexico, Southern U.S.)

- Hairless dog-like creature

- Mange-covered skin

- Hunched spine

- Sharp teeth and claws

- Often confused with coyotes or wild dogs

Some believe these are **two different creatures**.

Others say the Chupacabra is evolving.

Or worse... *multiplying*.

Theories and Speculation

No one knows what the Chupacabra really is.

Alien Experiment?

- The creature is too clean, too precise

- Some say it's an escaped alien hybrid or probe

Government Lab Experiment Gone Wrong?

- Puerto Rico has long-standing suspicions about secret military testing

- Some blame classified bioweapon research

Folklore Manifestation?

- Like La Llorona, Chupacabra may be born from fear—**a new monster for modern anxieties**

Rational Explanation?

- Many "sightings" are likely coyotes with mange
- But that doesn't explain the bloodless bodies
- Or the sheer **terror** reported by witnesses

Where It's Been Seen

Though born in Puerto Rico, the Chupacabra's legend has spread across:

- Mexico
- The Dominican Republic
- Chile
- Argentina
- The Southwestern United States (Texas, Arizona, New Mexico)

Anywhere rural. Anywhere dark. Anywhere the night is quiet enough to hear a flap of wings... or claws in the dirt.

Why It Took Hold

The Chupacabra exploded in the '90s—and not by accident.

It arrived at a moment of:

- Growing **mistrust in government**
- **Global alien obsession** (think *X-Files*)
- **Mass media panic**
- And a need to explain the unexplainable

It became a **catchall fear**:

When something went wrong in the night, it wasn't fate. It was **him**.

The Beast in Pop Culture

The Chupacabra is now *everywhere*:

- **Documentaries** on Discovery and History Channel
- **Scooby-Doo**, *South Park*, *X-Files* episodes
- **Goosebumps** and dozens of YA horror books
- **Memes, games, and podcast deep-dives**

Yet despite the coverage—**no one has ever caught it**.

No body. No DNA.

Just shadows. Dead animals. And fear.

- **Scare Rating:** 💀 💀 💀 💀
- **Truth Meter:** 🌑 Half cryptid, half hysteria
- **First Major Report:** March 1995, Canóvanas, Puerto Rico
- **Nickname:** "Goat-Sucker"
- **Modern Versions:** Canine (Texas) / Reptilian (Caribbean)

Final Words

They say it comes out when the moon is full.

They say it leaves no trace.

They say it doesn't need to bite—just *pierce and drain*.

So if you hear your animals panicking...

If you find lifeless bodies at dawn...

If the air feels *too still*—

It may not be hunger.

It may be **a warning**.

Because when Chupacabra feeds...

it never stops at just one.

Chapter 12
El Muerto (Texas/Mexico Border)

"They hanged him from his saddle. Now he rides with no head—and no mercy."

The sound of hoofbeats in the night.

No rider in sight.

Just dust... and dread.

Then you see it.

A horse galloping through the dark—wild-eyed, foaming at the mouth.

And strapped to the saddle...

a headless corpse swaying in the wind.

You've just seen **El Muerto**.

. . .

The Body That Wouldn't Stay Dead

The story begins in the **1800s**, on the lawless stretch of land between **South Texas and northern Mexico.**

Horse theft was rampant. And punishment was swift.

One thief—some say a bandit, others say a soldier turned outlaw—was finally caught after terrorizing the region. But the locals didn't just hang him.

They made a statement.

They **decapitated him**,

Strapped his body upright on a wild horse,

Tied his severed head to the saddle horn,

And **sent him riding** into the desert as a warning.

But the desert didn't bury him.

It **claimed him.**

And now, the horse returns on moonless nights—still carrying its rider.

Still headless.

Still riding.

The Ghost of the Borderlands

El Muerto is a **revenant**—a corpse that rides because justice wasn't finished.

Over time, the stories grew darker:

- Ranchers found livestock mutilated, hooves around the blood

- Travelers disappeared near old trails where the rider was last seen

- Gunshots fired at the horse hit nothing but air

- Dogs howled as if something passed them by—**something they couldn't see**

His head?

Still missing.

Maybe buried.

Maybe carried by crows.

Or maybe... he's looking for it.

Fact or Frontier Folklore?

There are **historical roots** to the legend.

A real outlaw named **Vidal** was captured and executed by Texas Rangers in the mid-1800s. His body was indeed tied to a horse and sent off to frighten other bandits.

But somewhere between history and horror, the tale grew teeth.

A corpse became a curse.

And now El Muerto isn't just a warning.

He's a **witness**.

To violence. To justice. To the brutal birth of the borderlands.

Where He Rides

Sightings stretch across:

- **South Texas ranchlands**
- **Northern Mexico** (Tamaulipas, Coahuila)
- Along forgotten trails, ghost towns, and old military roads

He appears especially during:

- **Storms**
- **Moonless nights**
- **Día de los Muertos** or after executions

Some claim he leaves hoofprints in solid rock.

Others swear they heard whispering—low, breathless—and a gurgling voice saying:

"Where is my head?"

Why He Endures

El Muerto is **vengeance in motion**.

He's what happens when justice goes too far—or not far enough.

He's the Wild West truth: that blood often repaid blood, and mercy was rare.

He also represents a **blurred boundary**:

- Between life and death
- Between justice and revenge
- Between history... and legend

- **Scare Rating:** 💀 💀 💀
- **Truth Meter:** 🪦 Historically based, embellished over time
- **Known Territory:** Texas-Mexico borderlands
- **Physical Clues:** Headless rider, black horse, bloodless bodies
- **Other Names:** "The Headless Horseman of South Texas"

Final Words

If you ever hear hooves pounding through the night...

If you feel the ground shake but see no rider...

If the wind smells like leather, dust, and decay—

Don't look.

Because some men ride even in death.

And some horses never stop running.

Mini-Feature: "Day of the Dead and the Blurring of Realms"

"They say the dead return for one night. But what if they never really left?"

In Mexico and parts of Latin America, there is one night where death does not divide us.

No screams. No shadows. No haunting.

Just candles. Bread. Marigolds. And names spoken aloud so the dead can find their way home.

It's called **Día de los Muertos**—*The Day of the Dead*.

And though it's wrapped in color and joy, beneath it flows a truth older than legend:

The dead are never far. And when the veil thins... they walk with us.

What Is Día de los Muertos?

It's not "Mexican Halloween." It's something deeper. Older.

Mini-Feature: "Day of the Dead and the Blurring of Realms"

Rooted in **Aztec beliefs** and blended with **Catholic traditions**, Día de los Muertos honors the departed—not with fear, but with celebration.

Over two nights—**November 1st (for children)** and **November 2nd (for adults)**—families build **ofrendas** (altars), filled with:

- Candles
- Pan de muerto (bread of the dead)
- Sugar skulls
- Favorite foods and drinks
- Photos of loved ones
- Bright **marigolds**, whose scent guides souls home

The idea is simple and powerful: **the dead come back.**

To eat. To laugh. To be remembered.

And if you welcome them, they leave in peace.

But Not All Spirits Are Peaceful

Most souls cross gently—joyfully.

But some?

They have **unfinished business**.

Legend says that during Día de los Muertos:

- **Spirits that died violently** may rise confused, even angry
- **Those forgotten** may feel lost, lingering too long

Mini-Feature: "Day of the Dead and the Blurring of Realms"

- **Those whose names are never spoken again** may become shadows—**without form, without rest**

In some rural towns, families leave offerings at **cemetery gates** to appease the wandering dead—those with **no altar of their own**.

The Blurring of Realms

Día de los Muertos is beautiful—but it's also **a doorway**.

And like all doorways, it can open the wrong way.

Some caution not to:

- Leave your altar unattended

- Speak to spirits unless you know their name

- Mock the dead or steal from a graveyard during the celebration

Because while the veil is thin... **so is the line between love and haunting.**

Pop Culture and the Afterlife

Films like *Coco* and *The Book of Life* introduced Día de los Muertos to global audiences, painting it as a world of color, music, and memory.

And they were right—*mostly.*

But those stories leave something out.

The **reverence**. The **risk**. The **quiet warnings** passed down in whispers.

Mini-Feature: "Day of the Dead and the Blurring of Realms"

Because Día de los Muertos isn't just about remembering.

It's about **being remembered**.

And what happens if you're not.

Why This Celebration Matters

More than any legend, Día de los Muertos reflects Latin America's core truth:

Death is not an end—it's a mirror.

One day you look in it... and someone you lost looks back.

Maybe with love. Maybe with longing.

But always watching.

And always waiting for **your voice** to call them home.

- **Theme:** Connection with the dead
- **Tone:** Sacred, joyful, yet eerie
- **Dates:** Nov 1–2
- **Traditions:** Ofrendas, cemetery visits, sugar skulls
- **Urban Legends:** Wandering souls, uninvited spirits, cursed altars
- **Scare Rating:** 💀 💀 (softly haunting)
- **Truth Meter:** Deep cultural belief, active tradition

Final Thought

This isn't a ghost story.

It's an invitation.

Mini-Feature: "Day of the Dead and the Blurring of Realms"

To speak the names of the dead.

To light candles not out of fear, but **faith**.

To remember that sometimes... the dead come not to haunt you, but to see if **you still remember them.**

And if you forget?

Well... that's when they start to cry.

Part 3

Europe – Haunted Roads and Vengeful Spirits

The fog clings longer here. The roads are older. The spirits are patient.

Chapter 13
The Vanishing Hitchhiker (UK)

"You pick her up. She gives you an address. But when you get there—she's already dead."

She's standing at the side of the road.

Alone. Pale. Soaked from the rain.

One hand raised. A quiet plea.

You slow down, wondering how long she's been out here.

She climbs in without a word.

You glance at her—she's young, maybe twenty. Dressed in something old-fashioned. A party dress, maybe? Or... funeral black?

She says only one thing:

"Can you take me home?"

You nod. Drive.

She doesn't speak again.

And when you pull into the driveway she gave you...

the seat beside you is empty.

The Story They Keep Telling

There are versions of this tale all over the world.

But in the UK, it's practically **national folklore**.

From **Essex to Edinburgh,** they tell of the girl on the roadside:

- Sometimes she's escaping a party.
- Sometimes she's trying to get to her mother.
- Sometimes she just stares straight ahead, silent.

And always, when the driver arrives—

She's gone.

They knock on the door, confused.

And the person who answers?

They just shake their head, eyes already wet.

"That's our daughter," they say.

"She died ten years ago. Right there on that road."

Where She Walks

You'll find her on lonely stretches of:

- The **A75** in Scotland
- The **Blue Bell Hill** near Kent
- Remote country lanes in Yorkshire and Surrey
- Nearly every dark road near an old graveyard or a bend with no guardrail

Drivers report:

- Sudden chills
- Fog rolling in unnaturally fast
- A voice that doesn't match the body
- Or worse: seeing her **after** they already passed the spot

Sometimes she's on the side of the road.

Sometimes, she's **already in the back seat.**

Why She Haunts

The stories say she died **in a car crash**.

Or was hit while hitchhiking.

Or was murdered by the driver she trusted.

She is unfinished. Unheard.

Trapped in the final moment of needing to get home—and never making it.

She repeats the journey, again and again.

Not for revenge. Not for rage.

But because she never knew she died.

The Psychology of the Passenger

This isn't just a ghost story.

It's a tale about **compassion**.

Obligation.

Strangers crossing paths in the dark.

The Vanishing Hitchhiker plays on:

- Fear of the unknown

- Guilt over helping too late

- The **awkward silence** between two people who should speak—but don't

And the horror?

It's subtle.

Soft.

The moment you realize you were talking to **someone who isn't there.**

A Legend That Travels

You'll find her in:

- The U.S. (Resurrection Mary, Chicago)
- France
- Japan (often at night on mountain roads)
- South Africa, Norway, and the Philippines

But the **British version** is often the most refined:

- Quieter
- Sadder
- More fog, less blood

She doesn't scream. She doesn't claw.

She simply **leaves.**

And something about that... is worse.

- **Scare Rating:** 💀 💀 💀
- **Truth Meter:** Widely reported, folkloric pattern
- **Key Locations:** Blue Bell Hill, A75 Kinmount, Epping Forest backroads
- **Variant Names:** The Ghost Passenger, The Roadside Lady, The Lost Girl
- **Modern Twist:** Dashcam stories, TikTok encounters, "phantom rider" clips

Final Words

Next time you're driving a long road at night—

And you see someone standing in the rain, alone—

You'll feel the urge to stop.

You'll roll down your window.

You'll hear the voice, soft and sad:

"Can you take me home?"

Say yes, if you must.

But whatever you do—**don't look in the mirror until you reach the driveway.**

Because if she's gone…

That's when she's real.

Chapter 14
The White Lady (Germany/Netherlands)

"She walks the ruins in white—forever waiting, forever watching."

You see her from the corner of your eye.

A figure in white, motionless among the trees.

Pale veil drifting in the wind.

A dress too clean for this earth.

She doesn't speak.

Doesn't chase.

Just stands there—watching you, as if she knows something you don't.

And when you look back a second time?

She's already gone.

• • •

A Spirit of Silence and Sorrow

She is called many names:

Die Weiße Frau. La Dame Blanche. De Witte Juffer.

The White Lady.

She is not one woman, but **a thousand echoes** of women—ghosts woven into the fabric of Europe.

You'll find her in:

- Crumbling **castles** and manor houses
- Abandoned **wedding halls** and garden paths
- Foggy **forest trails** and roadside ditches

Always in white.

Always alone.

Always **waiting**.

👰 Who Was She?

No one agrees. Everyone *thinks* they know.

Some say she was:

- A **noblewoman** locked away for forbidden love
- A **bride** who died on her wedding day
- A **mother** whose child vanished, or was stolen, or drowned
- A **witch**, executed and cursed to linger near her place of death

Sometimes she appears with sadness.

Sometimes with rage.

Sometimes... she just appears.

What She Does

The White Lady doesn't scream or chase.

But she leaves **tragedy** in her wake:

- A warning before someone dies
- A curse upon those who disturb her resting place
- A mirror of grief you didn't know you still carried

And in rare stories?

She speaks.

Not in words.

In feelings. In visions.

In a kind of pressure in the air that makes you remember **everything you tried to forget**.

Castles, Forests, and Faint Footsteps

Sightings span across **Europe**:

- **Germany**: Berlin's Babenhausen Barracks, Hohenzollern castles
- **Netherlands**: Veluwe forests, old estates in Gelderland

- **France, Switzerland, Poland**: Variants tied to ancient bloodlines

Common details:

- She glows faintly

- Her dress never touches the ground

- She never blinks

- And sometimes… she cries

If you hear the sobbing, you're already too close.

Symbolism of the White Lady

She represents:

- **Mourning frozen in time**

- **Feminine injustice**—especially tied to betrayal, control, and silence

- **Warnings** from the spirit world, especially about lineage, legacy, or land

She is **La Llorona** without the rage.

She is **Lady Macbeth** without the blood.

She is the **guilt that never died**.

Where She Lives Today

The White Lady still wanders:

- In **TikToks** filmed in castle ruins

- In **horror novels** about ghost brides and spectral mothers

- In **wedding folklore** (bad luck to wear all white twice, they say...)

- In **true haunting podcasts**, where listeners claim they met her—and their lives were never quite the same

She's not gone.

She's just **waiting for you to come closer**.

- **Scare Rating:** 💀 💀 💀 💀
- **Truth Meter:** 🧬 Folk archetype with centuries of sightings
- **Known Regions:** Germany, Netherlands, France, Austria, Poland
- **Key Traits:** Veiled, weeping, silent or sobbing, haunting high places
- **Alternate Names:** Dame Blanche, Die Weiße Frau, Witte Juffer, La Dama de Blanco

Final Words

They say if you see the White Lady once, she leaves you alone.

But if you see her **twice**... something is coming.

A death. A confession. A truth you've ignored for too long.

So next time you're exploring castle ruins, and you feel a chill —but hear nothing—

Don't follow the white figure into the dark.

Because what she's mourning... might be **you.**

Chapter 15
Krampus (Austria)

"He comes not with gifts, but with chains. Not with cheer, but with claws."

You hear the bells first.

Heavy, iron, dragging across cobblestone.

Then the clatter of hooves. The rattle of chains. A low, wet breathing—animal, but almost human.

It's snowing, but the air feels too hot. Like a furnace has opened beneath your feet.

You step out into the village square... and he's already there.

Tall. Horned. Furred.

Krampus.

Santa brings presents.

Krampus brings punishment.

The Monster Behind the Mistletoe

Long before Coca-Cola turned St. Nicholas into a jolly man in red, the people of the **Alps** feared something else that came in December.

Krampus is said to be:

- Half-goat, half-demon

- Covered in black or brown fur

- Sporting long horns, a forked tongue, and glowing yellow eyes

- Wearing chains and bells, dragging a sack or basket on his back

He doesn't climb chimneys. He doesn't say "ho ho ho."

He **beats bad children with birch sticks**.

And if they're really bad?

He stuffs them in his sack... and **takes them away.**

His Better Half: Saint Nicholas

Krampus doesn't work alone.

He is the **dark counterpart** to **St. Nicholas**:

- On **December 5th** (*Krampusnacht*), Krampus visits with Nicholas

- Good children get gifts from St. Nick

- Bad children get... him

In some stories, he only threatens.

In others, he follows through.

A knock at the door.

A rattling in the hall.

A scream... then silence.

Krampus in the Streets

In Austria and parts of Germany, the tradition lives on through **Krampuslauf** ("Krampus runs"):

- Young men dress as Krampus in terrifying, handcrafted masks

- They parade through towns, chase onlookers, and smack their legs with sticks

- Some carry torches. Some breathe fire. Some roam alleys alone, just to *be seen*

It's festive, yes.

But there's always a line of fear.

Even those who laugh nervously... don't turn their backs.

What Krampus Means

Krampus is more than a holiday boogeyman. He's a **moral specter**:

- A reminder that actions have consequences
- That winter isn't always warm
- That some spirits come not to give, but to **collect**

He represents:

- **Discipline** in dark times
- The **balance of light and shadow**
- A whisper that **not all traditions are soft and sweet**

Where He's Been—and Where He's Going

Though born in the Alps, Krampus has gone global:

- **U.S. Krampus runs** in cities like Philadelphia and Los Angeles
- Horror movies (*Krampus, A Christmas Horror Story*)
- **TikTok tutorials** on Krampus makeup and horns
- Holiday cards from the 1800s show him dragging children away—grinning

He is part of a growing movement to **reclaim the dark roots of winter.**

Because for most of history... **Christmas wasn't kind.**

It was survival.

Firelight.

Shadows pressing at the door.

And in those shadows—Krampus still waits.

- **Scare Rating:** 💀 💀 💀 💀 💀
- **Truth Meter:** 🌲 Deep folkloric roots, still practiced
- **Known Celebrations:** Austria, Bavaria, Slovenia, parts of Italy
- **Companions:** St. Nicholas, Perchta (another Alpine spirit)
- **Krampusnacht:** December 5th (night before St. Nick's Day)

Final Words

This holiday season, hang your stockings.

Pour your cider. Sing your songs.

But when the bells start ringing late at night...

When the wind smells like smoke and the footprints don't match the boots by the door...

Don't laugh too loudly.

Don't peek too long.

Because if you've been bad?

Krampus knows.

And he doesn't do coal.

Chapter 16

The Green Children of Woolpit (UK)

"They came from beneath the earth—green-skinned, wide-eyed, and full of secrets."

They were found near the edge of a wolf pit.

Two children. A boy and a girl.

Alone, lost, and **green**.

Their skin shimmered like spring leaves.

They spoke no known language.

They wore strange clothes made from unfamiliar cloth.

And they looked like they'd never seen the sun.

The villagers stood in silence, staring.

And the children stared back—terrified.

That was the summer Woolpit stopped feeling like part of England.

And started feeling like a place that touched something *else*.

The Year Was 1150

The village of **Woolpit**, in Suffolk, was quiet farmland surrounded by deep woods and old lore.

One day, reapers found the children near a **wolf pit**—a trap once used for hunting predators.

The children were crying, their skin **a pale green**, and they wouldn't eat.

Days passed before they accepted one thing: **raw broad beans**, eaten straight from the stalk.

Eventually, the girl began to speak.

The boy? He never adapted. He grew weaker... and died.

The Girl's Story

Once she learned English, the girl told a tale no one forgot:

"We came from a place with no sun.

Everything was dim, like twilight.

Everyone was green.

We followed a tunnel of sound... and ended up here."

She called it **St. Martin's Land**, where the light was low and the sun never rose.

They had been tending their father's animals when a strange noise—*like bells or a river*—pulled them through a cave.

When they emerged, they were in Woolpit.

Alone.

And wrong.

Were They... Human?

Centuries later, the story still defies explanation.

Some say:

- They were **fairy children**—lost from a hidden world beneath the hills

- Survivors from a **subterranean civilization**

- Orphans from **another planet**, caught in a slip between worlds

- Children of **Flemish immigrants**, hiding in the woods with chlorosis (a medical condition causing greenish skin)

But none of those explain:

- The strange language

- The clothes no one recognized

- The tunnel

- The sound

- The **green** that faded only after years of living under the real sun

What They Represent

The Green Children of Woolpit aren't a ghost story.

They're **a breach**—between logic and legend.

They embody:

- **Fear of the outsider**
- **A child's lens on the unknown**
- A quiet **terror of slipping between worlds and never getting home**

They are folklore's answer to a riddle science never solved.

And they've never gone away.

Modern Echoes

The Green Children have re-emerged in:

- **Sci-fi anthologies** and alien origin stories
- **Reddit threads** about dimensional rifts
- Podcasts and YouTube deep dives (*Unresolved, Stuff They Don't Want You To Know*)
- Modern theories tying them to **interdimensional travel**, **quantum anomalies**, and **parallel timelines**

But no matter the theory... no one explains them fully.

Because they weren't supposed to be explained.

They were supposed to **make you wonder**.

- **Scare Rating:** 💀 💀 💀
- **Truth Meter:** 🧬 Historical event with layers of folklore
- **First Accounted By:** Ralph of Coggeshall and William of Newburgh (12th century chronicles)
- **Location:** Woolpit, Suffolk, England
- **Theories:** Fairy realm, underground civilization, alien origin, famine refugees

Final Words

Sometimes, the monsters are obvious.

Sometimes, the ghosts are loud.

But sometimes... the story whispers.

Two children appear.

They don't belong.

And they disappear again—into history, into myth.

But if one day, while walking the woods, you hear music under the earth?

Don't follow it.

Because **not everyone who crosses the border between worlds gets to come back.**

Chapter 17
Spring-Heeled Jack (Victorian London)

"He leapt over walls, spat fire, and scratched with claws made of iron."

He came out of the fog.

Tall. Thin. Cloaked in black.

Eyes glowing red. Breath steaming like a furnace.

And before anyone could scream—he was gone.

Over rooftops. Over fences. Into legend.

He didn't just vanish—he **launched himself** into the night.

London would never forget him.

And neither would the women he left behind... **bleeding, screaming, or mad.**

. . .

The Terror Begins

The year was **1837**. London was stretching its limbs into the Industrial Age.

And something else was stretching too.

The first reports came from suburban neighborhoods:

- A girl attacked by a **leaping man** with **metal claws**

- A servant who answered the door and was met with **blue flames and laughter**

- A coachman's horse bolting in terror at a shadow that jumped over the cart—without touching the ground

The papers gave him a name that sounded like nonsense… but stuck:

Spring-Heeled Jack.

What Witnesses Described

Every encounter was strange—but had chilling consistency:

- **Clawed hands**, often described as metallic or mechanical

- **Eyes like red fire**

- A cape or cloak, sometimes a tight-fitting suit beneath

- Ability to **leap great distances**, often over tall gates or entire buildings

- In some cases—**he breathed fire or gas**, blinding and choking victims

And always: he vanished **without a trace.**

No footprints. No suspects. Just shadows.

Panic in the Papers

By 1838, Jack had become a **front-page fixture** in London newspapers.

And the attacks were growing:

- **Lucy Scales**, assaulted by a cloaked figure who spat blue flame in her face
- **Jane Alsop**, dragged into her doorway by a man claiming to be a police officer
  - She said he tore at her clothes with claws
  - And then vanished when her family ran to help

The fear was so widespread that:

- **Armed mobs** roamed London streets looking for him
- **Letters** poured into the Home Office demanding action
- Children whispered about him in alleyways and schoolyards

He had become the **boogeyman of the modern world.**

Theories, Hoaxes, and Hysteria

No one ever caught him. But theories bloomed like smog:

- A **deranged nobleman** with access to advanced technology

- A **stage magician** gone rogue

- An **escaped lunatic**

- An **early steampunk horror**, cobbled together by a city obsessed with crime and progress

Or maybe...

He was never real at all.

Just a case of mass hysteria.

Fueled by fear, fed by ink, grown in the dark.

But if that were true...

Why did he keep coming back?

Where He Walks Now

Spring-Heeled Jack didn't vanish with the fog.

He's been spotted in:

- **Liverpool (1904)**—witnesses said he leapt over rooftops like a frog

- **Aldershot barracks (1870s)**—terrifying British soldiers with inhuman jumps

- **Texas (1938)**—where newspapers reported a "leaping man in flames"

- Even on modern paranormal forums and YouTube comment sections

Every few decades, he reappears.

Same leap. Same claws. Same grin.

And then, just like that... he's gone again.

What He Means

Spring-Heeled Jack is **fear on the edge of reason**:

- A symbol of **urban anxiety**—the predator in the alley
- A personification of the **Industrial Age's speed and chaos**
- The first true **urban monster**—one built by newspapers, nightmares, and fog

He didn't just haunt streets.

He **haunted headlines**.

And no one ever proved he didn't exist.

- **Scare Rating:** 💀 💀 💀 💀
- **Truth Meter:** 🦴 Blended folklore, hoaxes, and hysteria
- **Known Haunts:** London, Liverpool, Midlands, possible U.S. sightings
- **Abilities:** Superhuman jumps, fire breathing, clawed attacks
- **Theories:** Prankster nobleman, ghost, alien, cryptid, mass hallucination

Final Words

Some say he was a trickster.

Some say a demon.

Some say he's just a story.

But next time you're walking alone through old London streets—

And you hear a rustle above you on the roof—

And the fog thickens faster than it should—

Don't stop.

Don't turn around.

And whatever you do...

Don't look up.

Because Spring-Heeled Jack only needs one leap.

Mini-feature: "Medieval Superstitions That Never Died"

"Knock on wood. Don't whistle at night. Cover the mirrors after death. Why? Because we still remember—even if we pretend not to."

They're just old sayings.

Harmless habits.

Traditions we don't question.

But deep down, we know... **they mean something.**

We don't walk under ladders.

We throw salt over our shoulders.

We still hang iron horseshoes, just in case.

These aren't quirks.

They're the **leftovers of a darker age**—when everyone believed in curses, omens, and the things that waited just outside the light.

Mini-feature: "Medieval Superstitions That Never Died"

And some of us still do.

The Witches' Mark and the Devil's Contract

In medieval Europe, fear of witches ran deep.

- People searched for **marks** on the body: moles, scars, or birthmarks said to be "devil's teats"

- Midwives and healers were especially vulnerable to accusation

- It was believed a witch could **curse your livestock** with a glance—or your child with a whisper

To protect yourself, you might:

- Draw **protective symbols** on your doorway

- Burn **rosemary** or **bay leaves**

- Bury **iron nails** beneath your threshold

Some still do.

The Evil Eye (Across Europe)

You've seen the charm: a blue glass eye, often hanging in a shop or sewn into clothes.

It's ancient. But still alive.

The **evil eye**—*malocchio*, *mati*, *ojo turco*—is the belief that certain gazes can:

- Cause illness

- Wilt crops

Mini-feature: "Medieval Superstitions That Never Died"

- Sour luck

- Dry up love

In:

- **Italy**, garlic was worn to repel it

- **Greece**, spitting (or pretending to) helped break its hold

- **Spain and Portugal**, children were "swept" with herbs to remove the curse

And today? You'll find evil eye charms on TikTok, Etsy, and in cars across Europe and the Mediterranean.

The Black Dog and the Death Omen

A large, black dog with glowing red eyes. Seen at night. Silent. Watching.

It was never just a stray.

It was a **harbinger of death**:

- In **England**, it's the Barghest or Black Shuck

- In **Ireland**, it's connected to **Cú Sídhe**, a fae hound from the Otherworld

- In **Germany**, it's tied to graveyards and crossroads

To see one means:

- You, or someone you love, will die soon

- Or that you've been marked—for something beyond this world

Mini-feature: "Medieval Superstitions That Never Died"

They still appear. Not in the news, but in stories told in low voices, after midnight.

Funeral Rites and Forbidden Mirrors

Death was dangerous.

Not just sad. Not just tragic. But **spiritually dangerous**.

To keep the dead from returning:

- **Mirrors were covered**—lest a soul get trapped

- **Clocks were stopped** at the moment of death

- **Chairs were turned over** to confuse spirits lingering in the home

- **Coins were placed on the eyes**, both to weigh them shut and as payment for the journey beyond

In rural parts of Europe, some of these rituals **still happen**.

Not out of fear...

But out of something deeper: **respect**.

Fairy Circles, Changelings, and the Forest Folk

Not all superstitions were about death.

Some were about **things older than death**.

- **Fairy circles** (rings of mushrooms) were thought to be dangerous portals

- **Changelings** were fae who swapped places with human infants—recognized by strange behavior or a sudden change in appearance

Mini-feature: "Medieval Superstitions That Never Died"

- In Wales, Ireland, and parts of Scandinavia, **offerings of bread and milk** were left to appease woodland spirits

These beliefs shaped how people planted, harvested, raised children, even traveled.

And in many places, they **still do**—quietly.

You just have to listen for them.

- **Themes:** Protection, curses, omens, rituals
- **Scare Rating:** 💀 💀 💀 (psychologically chilling)
- **Survival Today:** Evil eye charms, knocking on wood, mirror rituals, funeral superstitions
- **Why They Persist:** They're embedded in our *language*, *rituals*, and *memory*

Final Words

We tell ourselves we're modern.

We have electricity, medicine, maps.

But when the wind howls wrong, or the dog won't stop barking at nothing...

When a mirror cracks, or a figure vanishes just beyond the treeline...

We knock on wood.

We clutch the charm.

We whisper a prayer we don't quite believe.

Because superstition isn't weakness.

It's **ancestral survival, echoing through time**.

Part 4

Africa – Shadows, Warnings, and Witches

Here, legends do more than frighten—
they teach, protect, and remember

Chapter 18
Tokoloshe (South Africa)

"If your bed isn't raised by bricks, you're inviting it to climb in."

Something is in the room.

You can't see it—but you feel it.

The air is thick, too warm.

The blankets suddenly feel too heavy.

And then you hear it. Under the bed. At the edge.

Breathing.

You try to scream, but your voice won't work.

You try to move—but your arms are locked.

And just as sleep paralysis chokes you silent...

you feel something **pulling at your toes**.

. . .

They told you to raise your bed on bricks.

You didn't.

Now, the **Tokoloshe** has come.

Not Just a Monster—A Message

The Tokoloshe is one of the most feared figures in Southern African folklore.

It's not a ghost.

It's not a demon.

It's something **else**.

- Small. Hairy. Human-like, but wrong.
- Long fingers. Thick lips. Red, glowing eyes.
- Sometimes invisible.
- Always watching.

"He's like a goblin," people say.

But goblins don't **strangle you in your sleep.**

How It Works

The Tokoloshe is **summoned**.

Not born. Not wandering. **Sent.**

Usually by someone with a grudge—a witch, a rival, a neighbor with a hidden rage.

Once conjured, it's tasked to:

- Scare
- Harass
- Cause illness
- Drive people mad
- Or… kill

Especially at night.

Especially if you're sleeping on the floor.

That's why so many homes still raise beds on bricks or paint protective symbols by the doorway.

What It Wants

Some say it feeds on **fear**, others on **sexual energy**, still others on **death itself**.

In some stories:

- It sits on people's chests while they sleep
- It whispers lies in your ear until you go mad
- It drinks your breath, little by little, every night

In others:

- It's kept by witches as a **pet**

- Or as a **spiritual weapon**, passed down through bloodlines

It is not random.

It has a purpose.

And someone sent it.

Why the Beds Are on Bricks

In townships and villages across South Africa, beds are often raised off the ground—not for comfort, but for **protection**.

The Tokoloshe is **short**. If the bed is high enough, it can't reach you.

Even in modern urban homes, some families still quietly stack bricks under bed legs.

They don't always say why.

But they know.

Can You See It?

Most people can't. But:

- **Children** sometimes do—especially those near death
- **Elders** claim to feel it before it appears
- Dogs **bark at it**, but only when no one else is watching

It hides in shadows, behind curtains, under the sink, beneath your bed.

If your lights flicker.

If your dreams turn violent.

If your sleep begins to feel like drowning—

You may not be alone.

In Popular Culture

The Tokoloshe appears in:

- **South African horror films** (*The Tokoloshe*, 2018)
- **Urban legends** in townships and boarding schools
- **YouTube storytelling channels** and paranormal TikToks
- Even local crime reports, when death comes with no explanation

He is folklore—but he is also **present tense**.

A figure passed from whispers into headlines.

What the Tokoloshe Represents

The Tokoloshe is fear **personalized**.

He represents:

- **Envy**
- **Revenge**
- **Unspoken tension** in communities
- **Mental illness**, sleep paralysis, or grief that grows teeth

But more than that, he is a **cultural weapon**—used to warn, protect, and explain what people fear to say aloud.

He is a spirit made of shadow and purpose.

- **Scare Rating:** 💀 💀 💀 💀 💀
- **Truth Meter:** Active cultural belief, still feared
- **Known For:** Night attacks, strangulation, invisibility
- **Modern Echoes:** Raised beds, protective charms, psychological symbolism
- **Summoned By:** Witches, sangomas, enemies with deep rage

Final Words

You may not believe in him.

But next time you feel the air grow heavy in your room—

next time your chest won't move and your limbs refuse to listen—

next time your dreams turn to drowning and you wake up gasping—

Ask yourself this:

Did someone leave your bed too close to the ground?

Because **he only needs a little space**.

And once he climbs in...

he doesn't leave until he's done.

Chapter 19
Madam Koi Koi (Nigeria)

"Click… click… click. The heels echo first. Then the silence. Then the scream."

Everyone hears her before they see her.

The sound is soft at first.

One click. Then another.

Heels. In a hallway that should be empty.

Koi… koi… koi…

You freeze. It's past lights-out.

You're in your dorm bed, under the covers. The air is too still.

And the clicking is getting louder.

They told you about her.

Madam Koi Koi.

The teacher who died with blood on her shoes—and rage in her heart.

And now she walks.

Because no one said sorry.

Born in Boarding School Halls

Madam Koi Koi's legend is etched into the walls of **Nigerian boarding schools**, especially girls' schools.

There are many versions, but all start the same way:

She was once a **teacher**—elegant, strict, feared.

Always wore bright red heels.

She was proud of her shoes. Too proud.

Some say she was cruel—slapped students until they bled.

Some say the students **fought back** and she fell.

Others say **she was wronged**, pushed by staff, betrayed by the school.

Either way, she died.

And her shoes kept walking.

Why the Name?

The name comes from the sound:

- **Koi… koi… koi…**

The click of her red heels on concrete.

It's never hurried.

Never frantic.

Just steady. Controlled.

Like someone with **plenty of time**.

When She Appears

- **Late at night**, after lights-out
- In **bathrooms, hallways, empty classrooms**
- **Girls hear her** more often than boys
- She whispers names. Sometimes slaps. Sometimes just watches

You might hear her:

- Click past your dorm door
- Walk into your classroom after everyone leaves
- Whisper behind you at the sink—**when no one else is there**

Some say she leaves a faint smell of blood and perfume.

What She Does

Madam Koi Koi is unpredictable:

- In some stories, she drags girls away and they're never seen again

- In others, she just slaps you so hard you dream about it for days

- Some say she simply walks... until someone **looks her in the eye**

If you do?

You **don't sleep right again.**

Symbolism and Trauma

Madam Koi Koi is more than a ghost.

She is:

- A symbol of **abuse of power** in schools

- The **shame and silence** that follow trauma

- A product of **colonial-era discipline**, where humiliation and violence were normalized

She is **rage that was never heard.**

And so now, she walks the hallways of girls just trying to sleep, reminding them:

"You can't hide forever."

Modern Echoes

Madam Koi Koi lives on:

- In **urban legends** across Nigeria, Ghana, Uganda

- In **African horror anthologies** and school plays

- On **TikTok** and YouTube, where students act out her stories
- In whispered stories between generations of students—especially during exam week

She has become a **myth with memory**.

Everyone claims they've never seen her.

But everyone knows someone who has.

- **Scare Rating:** 💀 💀 💀 💀
- **Truth Meter:** 📚 Strong urban legend with roots in lived experiences
- **Known Haunts:** Nigerian boarding schools, especially girls' dorms
- **Core Sign:** Red heels clicking (the "koi koi" sound)
- **Common Warnings:** Don't be alone at night. Don't answer whispers. Don't disrespect her shoes.

Final Words

You might laugh at first.

She's "just a story," after all.

But when the halls are dark, and the other girls are asleep…

When you hear a single **click** from the hallway—

Don't move.

E.V. Nocturne

Don't breathe.

And for the love of everything—

Don't open the door.

Because **she's still angry.**

And she's walking...

just for you.

Chapter 20
Pinky Pinky (South Africa)

"She lives in the bathroom. She hates pink. And she's always hungry for girls who are alone."

You shouldn't have come in here alone.

The door creaked shut behind you.

The fluorescent light buzzes above your head.

The mirror's cracked. The stall is open. The silence is *wrong*.

And then you hear it.

Pinky Pinky... Pinky Pinky...

Whispered like a dare. Or a curse.

And now the door behind you won't open.

And something is crawling out from under the sink.

. . .

Born in School Bathrooms and Fear

Pinky Pinky is one of South Africa's most infamous urban legends.

She doesn't haunt forests or graves.

She haunts:

- **School restrooms**, especially in girls' bathrooms
- **Abandoned classrooms**
- **Changing rooms** after P.E.

Always where you're **vulnerable**.

Always where no one is watching.

Her targets?

Girls who wear pink.

What She Looks Like

Descriptions change. But the dread doesn't.

Some say:

- She has **one leg**, twisted
- Her eyes are huge, white, and staring
- Her nails are claws, and her skin is stretched too tight
- Underneath it all—**she may be a man** wearing a girl's skin

She's sometimes half-human, half-monster.

Sometimes dressed in pink.

Sometimes bloodstained.

Always wrong.

What She Does

She **attacks** girls in bathrooms—especially those alone.

- Drags them into empty stalls
- Scratches them until they bleed
- Leaves them passed out, shaken, or missing
- Sometimes... they don't come back

And if you wear pink underwear?

That's said to **draw her out**.

Some girls say she **asks questions** before she hurts you:

"Why do you wear pink?"

"Do you think you're pretty?"

"Do you think anyone's coming to help?"

And then she laughs.

What She Means

Pinky Pinky is **not just a ghost**.

She is a **manifestation of gender-based fear**:

- Fear of assault

- Fear of being alone and unprotected
- Fear of being punished for simply existing in a girl's body

She appeared during **post-apartheid South Africa**, when schools were changing, but the danger remained.

She is the **trauma no one reported.**

The violence hidden in plain sight.

The reason some girls stopped wearing pink at all.

Why Bathrooms?

The bathroom is **private.**

But for girls, it's often where they feel **most exposed.**

- It's where bullying happens
- Where they're watched
- Where fear lives when teachers aren't around

Pinky Pinky turns the bathroom into a **hunting ground.**

She's not chasing attention.

She's chasing silence.

Modern Echoes

Pinky Pinky lives on through:

- **Spoken warnings** in schools—especially among girls
- **South African horror fiction** and short films

- **TikTok videos** recreating "real" sightings

- Local media stories where attacks are blamed on something inhuman

She's also used in **feminist horror writing**—a symbol of what girls are told to ignore.

Because the scariest thing about Pinky Pinky?

She might not be supernatural at all.

- **Scare Rating:** 💀 💀 💀 💀
- **Truth Meter:** 👁 Real cultural fear, wrapped in folklore
- **Known Locations:** Johannesburg, Cape Town, Durban schools
- **Triggers:** Pink clothing, being alone, bathrooms
- **Common Advice:** Never go alone. Don't answer if she whispers. Don't wear pink under your uniform.

Final Words

You may laugh when they tell you the story.

You may say "monsters aren't real."

But when you walk into the bathroom alone—

And the stall door creaks open by itself—

And you see two bare feet under the sink, facing the wrong way—

Just hope you're not wearing pink.

Because **Pinky Pinky is real to the ones she's already taken.**

And she's always looking for **the next girl to disappear.**

Chapter 21
The Adze (Ghana / Togo)

"You think it's just a firefly. But when you wake up weak, and your dreams feel hollow—you've been visited."

You swat at something near your ear.

A tiny flicker of light. Maybe a bug. Maybe nothing.

But then you feel it—your skin is cold.

You're sweating. Breathing harder.

Your chest feels caved in.

You wake up in the morning dizzy, tired, as if something has **taken something from you** in the night.

You check the room.

There's no bite.

But in the shadows near your window, a faint glow fades.

They say it came while you slept.

The Adze.

A Spirit in Insect's Skin

In **Ewe folklore** (from Ghana, Togo, and Benin), the **Adze** is a shape-shifting creature that feeds on **life energy**.

It often takes the form of a **firefly**—harmless, glowing, almost beautiful.

But it's a disguise.

The Adze enters homes through cracks, keyholes, or windows.

It lands on the skin of a sleeping victim—**usually a child or the vulnerable**—and drains them slowly.

You never wake up in time.

You just grow weaker.

And eventually, you waste away.

Its Human Form: The Witch Within

The Adze is more than a parasite—it has a **human side**.

If captured or killed in firefly form, it turns into a **human witch**—someone known to the community.

That's when the real fear starts:

- A neighbor
- A relative

- Someone you always suspected... but never had proof

Witch trials weren't always for drama.

They were **the desperate answer** to someone who couldn't be explained.

Why It Comes

The Adze doesn't kill for fun.

It feeds on:

- **Jealousy**
- **Bitterness**
- **Unspoken rage**

Some believe it's **summoned** by those who envy your success, beauty, or luck.

Others say it's a spirit of **revenge**—targeting those whose families have caused harm, even generations ago.

In many villages, unexplained sickness—especially in children—is still quietly blamed on it.

Signs of an Adze Attack

- Sudden fatigue or sickness without medical cause
- Nightmares involving insects, suffocation, or glowing light
- Dying crops or animals near the house
- Children waking up screaming—then getting quiet, too quiet

You might not see it.

But someone always suspects.

And once it starts... it rarely stops on its own.

What the Adze Represents

The Adze is:

- **Sickness as spirit**

- **Envy given wings**

- A way to explain what modern medicine once couldn't

It's the fear that what harms us most isn't foreign—it's **familiar**.

And that something as small as a firefly can carry centuries of **unspoken grief and guilt**.

Modern Reflections

The Adze appears in:

- **African horror fiction**, often as a metaphor for inherited trauma

- **Contemporary witchcraft cases** in West Africa

- Paranormal **documentaries and podcasts**, exploring its overlap with sleep paralysis and disease

- Urban retellings—where fireflies near hospitals or orphanages aren't seen as pretty... but as warnings

It hasn't faded.

It's just gotten harder to swat.

- **Scare Rating:** 💀 💀 💀 💀
- **Truth Meter:** Deep traditional belief, tied to health and social tensions
- **Shape:** Firefly by night; human by day
- **Known Regions:** Ewe communities in Ghana, Togo, Benin
- **Defenses:** Nets, sealed windows, fire, confession rituals

Final Words

So the next time you see a firefly flicker past your window at night—

Don't open it.

Don't chase the light.

And don't assume it's just another bug.

Because some things glow not to guide you...

but to feed on what makes you human.

And once the Adze finds your skin?

It always comes back for more.

Chapter 22
The Night Whistler (Kenya)

"If you hear whistling at night... pretend you didn't. Don't look out the window. Don't speak. And whatever you do—don't whistle back."

It always begins the same way.

A single note, drifting through the night air.

Sharp. Clear. Familiar.

Whhheeet...

You pause.

It could be someone walking home.

A farmer. A watchman. A bored neighbor.

But then it comes again.

Whhheeet... whhheeet...

Too close.

Too steady.

And still—**no footsteps.**

They say if you answer...

you've just agreed to something.

And you won't realize **what** until it's already too late.

A Spirit That Calls, Not Chases

The **Night Whistler** is a ghost story passed in whispers across parts of **Kenya**, **Tanzania**, and **Uganda**.

Unlike monsters with claws or glowing eyes, this one is **invisible**.

It doesn't scream or growl.

It doesn't knock.

It **whistles**.

A calm, calculated tune.

Sometimes a song you recognize.

Sometimes your own name, in rhythm.

It doesn't need to break in.

It just needs you to answer.

. . .

What It Wants

Stories vary, but the fear is always the same:

- It's a **spirit of the forgotten**, calling out to be noticed
- It's a **shapeshifter**, hunting by mimicry
- It's **an omen**—your name whistled before your death
- Some say it's a **lost soul**, looking for company

The rules are simple:

- Never **whistle at night**
- Never **respond to the whistle**
- Never **say your name after dark**

Because once it knows you...

It starts to **follow**.

How It Moves

It doesn't bang or scratch.

It circles.

- First, it whistles from a distance.
- Then, closer.
- Then... *under your window.*

It may whistle your **language**, your **hometown melody**, or the lullaby your mother used to hum.

That's how it gets in.

Not through doors.

Through memory.

Who It Finds

Victims are often:

- Children who whistle before bed

- People walking alone at dusk

- Those who speak their name aloud after dark

- Anyone foolish enough to say, "I'm not afraid of the Whistler"

He doesn't need much.

Just a moment of attention.

A single note of acknowledgment.

And then—**you're marked.**

What the Whistler Represents

The Night Whistler is a ghost born from:

- **Loneliness**

- **Grief**

- **The consequences of breaking quiet traditions**

It reminds us that **not everything that calls you wants to be found.**

That some sounds were made to be **ignored**.

And that sometimes, silence isn't just safe—

It's **sacred**.

Modern Appearances

The Night Whistler appears in:

- East African **oral storytelling circles**
- Modern **folk horror podcasts** and Reddit tales
- Superstitions shared by **grandparents**, especially in rural areas
- Night watchmen stories: "I heard something call me by name… but no one was there."

Even in cities, the warning survives:

"If you whistle at night, you're whistling *back* at something."

- **Scare Rating:** 💀 💀 💀 💀 💀
- **Truth Meter:** Regional folklore with strong behavioral roots
- **Known Regions:** Kenya (Kikuyu, Luo), Tanzania, Uganda
- **Key Trait:** Whistling that mimics, moves, or lingers
- **Common Rules:** Don't whistle after sunset. Don't respond to your name. Don't answer unfamiliar tunes at night.

Final Words

It might be nothing.

Just the wind. Just the trees. Just a bird in the dark.

But if it whistles...

And it doesn't stop...

And it sounds like something *you've heard before—*

Do **not** look out the window.

Do **not** say your name.

And above all—

Do **not** whistle back.

Mini-feature: "Fear and Folklore in Colonial Contexts"

"When power came wearing boots and borders, the stories changed. But the spirits never left."

They say African spirits are old.

But some are newer than we think.

Some were born **after the borders** were drawn.

After languages were renamed.

After schools were built and gods were rebranded.

These are not just ghost stories.

They are **resistance stories**.

They are the whispers of cultures forced underground.

The memory of fear passed from child to child.

The **echo of violence**, reshaped until it could speak again—through monsters, witches, and warnings.

Mini-feature: "Fear and Folklore in Colonial Contexts"

Madam Koi Koi: Ghost of the Classroom

She walks the tile hallways of girls' schools—**a relic of colonial discipline**.

- Her story spread as **Western-style boarding schools** took root in Nigeria

- These schools taught silence, obedience, and shame

- Her ghost walks as a **symbol of rebellion**, grief, and forgotten justice

She may be fictional.

But the fear she carries? **Very real.**

The Tokoloshe: Born of Inequality

The Tokoloshe rose in townships where:

- Beds were low

- Windows were broken

- Fear moved faster than electricity

The creature punished vulnerability.

Pinky Pinky and Anxiety

She showed up in restrooms—but she came from somewhere deeper.

- During South Africa's transition to democracy, schools changed—but violence didn't disappear

- Pinky Pinky targeted **girls**, especially those just entering puberty

Mini-feature: "Fear and Folklore in Colonial Contexts"

- The legend became a way to **name unspoken dangers**: assault, body-shaming, gender policing

She is the thing no adult will explain, but every girl is warned about.

The Adze and Colonial Medicine

In Ghana and Togo, the Adze was long feared for its invisible attacks:

- Illness. Madness. Wasting disease.

But during colonial rule, **European doctors** often dismissed these beliefs—offering pills without understanding the **spiritual context**.

For many, the Adze was a **spiritual diagnosis** that medicine could not touch.

Fear became both explanation… and protection.

Why the Whistler Still Calls

Even after independence, even in cities with lights and laws— **the Whistler still comes.**

Because colonialism may have changed maps…

but it didn't erase **the belief that danger listens when you speak carelessly.**

Some things are older than language.

Older than fear.

Some things are **watching**.

Mini-feature: "Fear and Folklore in Colonial Contexts"

- **Theme:** Folklore born from history and trauma
- **Common Threads:** Authority, silence, identity, gender
- **Legends Affected:** Tokoloshe, Madam Koi Koi, Pinky Pinky, Adze
- **Modern Legacy:** Ongoing in schools, villages, storytelling, and urban legends
- **Scare Rating:** 💀 💀 💀 (haunting by context, not jumpscares)

Final Thought

Colonialism took land, names, gods.

But the stories? They slipped through the cracks.

Changed form. Hid in whispers. Survived in symbols.

So when we tell African ghost stories today, we're not just telling tales.

We're **remembering**.

We're **resisting**.

And we're keeping a promise:

That no spirit—no pain, no name—will ever be fully forgotten.

Part 5

Asia – Spirits in Mirrors, Games, and Alleys

You don't summon these spirits—they're already watching.

Chapter 23
Kuchisake-onna (Japan)

"She steps out of the shadows and asks you a question. There is no right answer. Only how long it takes her to kill you."

You're walking home after dark.

The street is empty. The wind cuts through your jacket.

You hear footsteps behind you—soft, deliberate, matching your pace.

You glance over your shoulder.

A woman is following.

She's wearing a **trench coat**, and a **surgical mask** over her face.

She walks faster.

You walk faster.

Then she's in front of you.

Blocking your path. Tilting her head. Her voice is gentle, almost kind:

"Am I pretty?"

The Wrong Question

If you say **no**—she pulls out a **knife** and kills you.

If you say **yes**—she removes the mask.

Her mouth is **slit ear to ear**, a ragged smile torn across her face.

"How about now?" she whispers.

If you scream, run, lie, pray—it won't matter.

She always wins.

Because the question is a **trap**.

And you were already **too close**.

A Legend Reborn

Kuchisake-onna means **"Slit-Mouthed Woman."**

Her story has been passed through Japan for **centuries**—but in 1979, she returned.

For real.

Across Japan, reports came flooding in:

- Students being followed

- Police put on patrol outside schools

- Teachers forming escort groups to get kids home

- People claiming to see a **masked woman** asking strangers if they thought she was beautiful

Newspapers called it **mass hysteria**.

But the fear was very real.

And she's never gone away.

Where She Comes From

There are many origin stories. None of them kind.

- A woman who was **vain**, obsessed with her beauty

- Her husband—jealous or angry—**slit her mouth open** to punish her

- "Now no one will ever say you're beautiful again," he said

In death, she returns—still obsessed with beauty, but **twisted** by pain.

Other versions say:

- She was disfigured in an accident

- A failed surgery

- A curse

- A victim of war or a botched cosmetic procedure

But no matter the past—her **future is yours.**

. . .

How to Survive Her

They say she still wanders **quiet alleys**, **suburban streets**, even **shopping malls** late at night.

If you're unlucky enough to meet her, there are only a few tricks to escape:

• Say "**You're average.**" (Not good, not bad. Just enough to confuse her.)

• Distract her with **candy** or **money**

• Ask her **a question in return**—to buy time and run

• Carry **pomade** (hair gel). For some reason, she hates the smell.

But these aren't guarantees.

They're **superstitions**.

Because once she asks you **the question**...

"Am I pretty?"

She already knows what she's going to do.

What She Represents

Kuchisake-onna is more than a horror story.

She's a reflection of **modern anxieties** wrapped in ancient fear.

She is:

• The danger behind **feminine beauty standards**

- **Punishment for vanity**, or a woman wronged by violence

- A ghost weaponized by a **society that never lets women win**

Say she's beautiful? You're shallow.

Say she's ugly? You're cruel.

Say nothing?

You're already bleeding.

Modern Echoes

You'll still find her:

- In **Japanese horror films** like *Carved* and *Kuchisake-onna*

- In **cosplay** and **TikToks** across Asia and beyond

- In **schoolyard whispers**, where kids still warn each other not to talk to strangers in masks

She's even crossed into **American urban legend** circles now.

YouTube creators remake her story every year.

Because she's simple.

And she's terrifying.

And anyone who's ever been asked, "Do I look okay?"— knows why.

- **Scare Rating:** 💀 💀 💀 💀 💀
- **Truth Meter:** 🔪 Widely believed during the 1979 panic, now urban legend with deep roots
- **Signature Phrase:** "Am I pretty?" / "How about now?"
- **Weaknesses:** Candy, pomade, wordplay
- **Cultural Role:** Commentary on beauty, trauma, social pressure

Final Words

You may laugh at the story now.

You may roll your eyes at the idea of a ghost in a face mask.

But the next time you turn a corner late at night—

And a woman in a long coat steps in front of you—

And she's wearing a mask, and holding something sharp—

And she asks,

"Am I pretty?"

Don't answer.

Just **run.**

Chapter 24
The Elevator Game (Korea)

"Push the buttons in the right order, and the elevator won't take you where you want to go. It'll take you somewhere else. Somewhere you were never meant to find."

You find a building.

It's late. Quiet. Ten stories or more. Perfect.

You enter alone.

Press the button. Step inside.

And then—**you begin.**

- 4th floor
- 2nd
- 6th
- 2nd again

- 10th

- 5th...

Don't speak. Don't let anyone in.

Don't look up if a woman enters.

If you've done it right... the elevator won't stop at the 10th floor.

It'll keep going.

And when the doors open again, you won't be in your world anymore.

The Ritual

The **Elevator Game** is a modern urban legend and ritual that originated in **South Korea**, then spread through **internet forums**, creepypasta sites, Reddit, and LINE chat horror stories.

It's said to take you to **another dimension**—a cold, empty version of reality where no one else exists.

But getting back isn't guaranteed.

The rules are strict:

- You must be alone

- The building must have at least **10 floors**

- You must press the floor buttons in **precise order**

- If someone else enters: **start over**

And if a woman walks in on the **5th floor—do not speak to her**.

Do not **look at her**.

Even if she looks familiar.

Even if she cries.

Even if she whispers your name.

What Happens on the Other Side

If you make it to the final step, the elevator will take you to the **10th floor**.

The doors open... but everything is off.

- The sky is red
- The building looks the same, but **feels wrong**
- Electronics don't work
- You feel like you're being watched
- There are **no people**

Some say it's a **parallel world**.

Others say it's a **trap**, and you were **never supposed to find it**.

If you stay too long, you might forget:

- Who you are
- Why you came

- How to get back

And if you speak to the woman?

You never leave.

What the Game Represents

The Elevator Game is **ritual horror**—but also a **metaphor**.

It speaks to:

- **Escapism**: the desire to leave our world behind

- **Loneliness**: the fantasy of being alone—until you are

- **Curiosity punished**: the fear that knowing too much opens doors we can't close

It's a **personal apocalypse**, quiet and slow.

And worst of all? **You chose it.**

How It Spread

The Elevator Game became internationally famous after:

- A series of viral **Reddit creepypasta posts**

- Horror **YouTube videos** with re-enactments

- The **Elisa Lam case (2013)**, where conspiracy theorists linked her death to this ritual

- **Korean blogs and message boards** in the early 2000s

Now, it's a **digital folklore ritual**, shared across TikTok, Discord, and gaming streams.

Some people still try it.

Most don't finish.

And those who say they succeeded?

They don't talk much anymore.

If You Want to Try It...

(You shouldn't. But here's how.)

Step sequence (may vary slightly online):

1 Enter the elevator on the 1st floor.

2 Go to 4th → 2nd → 6th → 2nd → 10th → 5th.

3 A woman may enter on 5. Don't look. Don't speak.

4 Press 1. If the elevator starts going to 10 instead... the ritual worked.

5 On the 10th floor, step out **only if you're sure you're alone**.

6 To return: Repeat the button sequence in **reverse**, then exit on **exactly the right floor.**

Mess up?

You might ride the elevator forever.

- **Scare Rating:** 💀 💀 💀 💀
- **Truth Meter:** ▰ Internet-born legend, widely reported online
- **Core Fears:** Isolation, trap dimensions, faceless women
- **Similar Rituals:** Red Room (Japan), Daruma-san game, 3 Kings (U.S. internet ritual)
- **Tools Required:** Elevator, courage, strict silence, total control

Final Words

It's just a game.

That's what you'll tell yourself.

Until the elevator doors slide open…

and the world outside is **empty**.

And the woman is smiling.

And you remember that **you came here alone.**

And now?

You're not alone anymore.

Chapter 25
Nale Ba (India)

"She comes at night. She calls your name. If you open the door, someone dies. If you want to live—tell her to come tomorrow."

It begins with a knock.

Not loud. Just enough.

A soft, rhythmic tap at the door.

You're alone. It's well past midnight.

You shouldn't hear anyone.

Then—your name.

"Amit…"

"Meena…"

"Open the door."

A voice you know. A friend. A relative.

Maybe even your mother.

But you remember what the neighbors said.

You remember the chalk writing scratched above your doorframe:

Nale Ba. Come Tomorrow.

And tonight...

you don't answer.

The Ghost at the Door

The **Nale Ba** legend comes from **Karnataka**, South India— particularly from **Bangalore** in the 1990s.

People began to report strange deaths:

- A healthy person dies in their sleep
- A newlywed man collapses without cause
- A child disappears after answering a midnight knock

Rumors spread fast.

The cause?

A **churel**. A **witch**. A **spirit bride**.

No one knew for sure.

But everyone agreed on one thing:

She comes at night.

She knocks.

She calls your name.

And if you answer—**someone dies.**

The Power of the Phrase

The solution was simple. Chillingly simple.

People began writing **Nale Ba (ನಾಳೆ ಬಾ)** in chalk on their front doors and compound walls.

It means:

"Come Tomorrow."

And for some reason...

She listens.

Not because she's kind.

Because she follows **rules**.

She returns. Night after night.

But never comes in.

Not if the writing is there.

Who Is She, Really?

The spirit is different in every version:

- A **bride** who died on her wedding night

- A **vengeful ghost woman** seeking men to claim as husbands

- A **demon** drawn to children and the elderly

- A **widow**, wronged, disfigured, abandoned

Some say she takes the form of someone you love.

Others say you never see her face at all—just **hear the knock**, the voice, the invitation.

She doesn't break in.

You must **let her in**.

And if you do?

She doesn't just take you.

She takes **someone you love**.

What the Legend Means

Nale Ba isn't just a superstition—it's **ritual defense**.

She represents:

- The fear of **loss without reason**

- **Widow ghosts**—a recurring theme in Indian folklore

- Urban panic during times of **unexplained tragedy**

- The idea that **you can outsmart death**... if you know what to write

She is every unsolved mystery, every tragic coincidence, **personified**.

Real-World Panic

In the 1990s:

- Entire **neighborhoods** wrote "Nale Ba" on their doors
- **Chalk was sold out** in local markets
- Children were kept inside after dark
- Some **villages declared curfews**

To this day, in rural parts of India, you can still see faded "Nale Ba" scrawled on crumbling walls.

A ghost turned into a **graffiti spell**.

A whisper turned into a wall.

Pop Culture Echoes

Nale Ba lives on in:

- The **Bollywood horror film** *Stree* (2018), which modernized the story with comedy and fear
- **YouTube horror channels** that document live recreations
- Urban legends shared on Indian TikTok and WhatsApp
- Schoolchildren still daring each other to knock three times and call her name

She's not forgotten.

She's **waiting.**

- **Scare Rating:** 💀 💀 💀 💀
- **Truth Meter:** 🧂 Based in mass panic with deep folkloric roots
- **Known Region:** Karnataka, India (especially Bangalore)
- **Defense:** "Nale Ba" chalked or written above the door
- Varia

nts: Ghost bride, cursed widow, demon caller

Final Words

You hear the knock again.

You want to check. Just to be sure.

But then the voice comes—

"Open the door. It's me."

And something inside you goes cold.

You pick up the chalk. Write the words again.

Nale Ba. Come Tomorrow.

And hope to God...

she doesn't forget how to read.

Chapter 26
Pontianak (Malaysia/Indonesia)

"She smells like frangipani and rot. Her laugh is high and wrong. If you hear her in the trees—it's already too late."

It starts with the flowers.

The scent drifts through the air—sweet, heavy, sticky.

Frangipani.

You look around. It's night. There shouldn't be any blooming trees nearby.

And then you hear her laugh.

High.

Breathy.

Too loud.

Too close.

You run.

But she was never behind you.

She's already in front of you.

The Woman Who Died Wrong

The **Pontianak** is one of Southeast Asia's most feared spirits.

She is said to be:

- A woman who **died during childbirth**, or while pregnant
- Her soul, filled with pain and rage, became corrupted
- She rises as a **vengeful spirit**, forever hunting

In life, she was silenced.

In death, she **screams**.

She is **terrifyingly beautiful**—until she isn't.

What She Looks Like

By day, she may appear as:

- A **pale, graceful woman**
- Long **black hair**
- A white dress or shroud
- Red eyes, if you get too close

By night:

- Her nails grow long and sharp
- Her mouth tears open to feed
- Her voice **distorts** into something inhuman

She rides the wind.

Appears in palm trees.

Or simply materializes behind you, **already reaching out.**

What She Does

The Pontianak is **not subtle**.

She:

- Preys on **men**, especially unfaithful, violent, or cruel ones
- Can smell **blood**, **fear**, or the scent of recent birth
- Uses **laughter** to lure or paralyze her victims
- **Disembowels** with her nails or teeth

Some say she drinks **blood**.

Others say she eats **organs**—starting with the **eyes**.

You may feel her cold breath on your neck before you ever see her.

And by then, it's far too late.

Where She Walks

The Pontianak is told in:

- **Malaysia**, **Indonesia**, and **Singapore**

- Rural roads, forest paths, and coconut plantations

- Places with tragic histories or where **young women died in pain**

She's also associated with:

- **Street corners where people vanish**

- **Abandoned homes**

- **Gravesites where no one visits anymore**

In Pontianak, Indonesia—yes, the city bears her name—there are still people who avoid going out after midnight.

Especially if they smell flowers on the wind.

How to Protect Yourself

There are few ways to stop her:

- Drive a **nail into the nape of her neck**—it's said to turn her docile or human

- Carry **nails, garlic,** or **sacred charms**

- Avoid wandering alone at night, especially in places where **someone has died recently**

But truly?

She cannot be stopped.

Only **postponed**.

. . .

What She Represents

The Pontianak is vengeance wrapped in grief.

She is:

- A woman denied dignity in death

- The embodiment of **feminine rage**—violent, righteous, supernatural

- A symbol of how **women's suffering becomes legend**, rather than justice

She is not just a ghost.

She is **every scream that wasn't heard in time**.

Modern Sightings

The Pontianak appears in:

- Malaysian and Indonesian horror films (*Kuntilanak, Pontianak Harum Sundal Malam*)

- Local short films and viral TikToks

- Internet maps marking "haunted roads" where she's been seen

- Schoolyard dares: knock on a tree and whistle, and she'll come

She never really disappeared.

She just learned to follow **cars instead of carriages**.

- **Scare Rating:** 💀 💀 💀 💀 💀
- **Truth Meter:** 💧 Deep folklore still feared in many regions
- **Haunts:** Forests, trees, crossroads, birth-related deaths
- **Tell-Tale Signs:** Frangipani scent, laughter, red eyes, sudden chill
- **Related Figures:** Kuntilanak (Indonesia), Sundel Bolong (another backless spirit)

Final Words

You smell something floral. Sweet. Familiar.

And the hairs on your neck rise.

You turn too late.

She's already there.

Not crying. Not asking.

Just **laughing**.

And the last thing you see is white silk, and nails like knives.

Because the Pontianak doesn't haunt.

She hunts.

Chapter 27
Jikininki (Japan)

"They were selfish in life. In death, they feast on corpses. And they know what they've become."

You pass an old temple at the edge of town.

It's dusk. The wind is heavy. The doors are open.

No one greets you. No chants. No prayers. Just incense—**too thick**.

And then you see it.

A figure hunched in the shadows.

Face twisted, eyes glowing faintly.

Gnawing on something you can't see—yet.

You realize you're near a **fresh grave**.

And it's not the only one.

. . .

The Corpse-Eaters of the Afterlife

In Japanese Buddhist folklore, there is a specific kind of ghost called a **Jikininki** (食人鬼)—literally, "**human-eating spirit.**"

They weren't murderers.

They weren't cursed by others.

They were cursed by **themselves**.

Because in life, they were:

- Greedy

- Selfish

- Spiritually corrupt

- Obsessively attached to **wealth or status**

When they died, their soul became twisted.

And their punishment?

Eternal hunger.

But only for **dead bodies**.

What They Are

Jikininki look **almost human**, from a distance.

But when you get closer:

- Their skin is waxy, corpse-like

- Their mouths are torn too wide

- They emit the smell of death and old incense
- Their **teeth are too many**—and always wet

They only come out at night.

They're drawn to funerals, roadside accidents, fresh burials.

They hide.

They wait.

They feed.

And then, they weep.

The Curse of Awareness

Unlike most monsters, **Jikininki know what they are**.

They hate themselves.

They're ashamed.

But the hunger is stronger than the guilt.

After feeding, they sob.

They pray.

Some try to warn travelers to stay away.

They are **ghosts trapped in a loop of punishment**:

- Feed
- Regret
- Feed again

They can't stop.

Not until someone performs a ritual to release them.

And few ever do.

How the Legend Survived

Jikininki appear in:

• **Buddhist texts** and **monk stories**, passed down over generations

• **Lafcadio Hearn's 1904** collection *Kwaidan*, which brought the story to English readers

• **Tales of wandering monks** who stumble into temples of death

They are part of a broader Japanese belief in **spiritual balance**:

• Good deeds and intention = peaceful death

• Selfishness = corruption beyond the grave

They're not evil.

They're **trapped**.

What They Represent

Jikininki are more than horror—they're **moral consequence**.

They represent:

• Fear of **dying with regret**

- The cost of spiritual neglect

- Guilt you can't outrun, even after death

- A caution against **greed**, **vanity**, and living without compassion

They're not here to punish others.

Only themselves.

But you're still in danger—because **you're what they crave.**

Modern Adaptations

Though lesser known than other Japanese ghosts, Jikininki appear in:

- **Anime and manga** (like *Hell Girl*, *Mushishi*, *Bleach*)

- **Japanese horror films** that mix Buddhism with gore

- **Creepypasta adaptations** that reframe them as cannibalistic ghouls

- Haunted temple stories passed through regional folklore

And every once in a while...

Someone still finds a **temple with no monks.**

Just incense.

And something that moves in the dark.

- **Scare Rating:** 💀 💀 💀
- **Truth Meter:** Classical Buddhist folklore
- **Known Traits:** Cannibalism of the dead, shame, rotting appearance
- **Haunts:** Graveyards, temples, sites of death
- **Can They Be Freed?:** Only by powerful monks or ritual compassion

Final Words

You see the figure kneeling by the grave.

You think it's praying.

Then it turns, and you see what's in its hands.

It stares at you—not angry. Not hungry. Just… ashamed.

And then it vanishes into the mist, dragging the body with it.

Because the Jikininki doesn't want you.

It wants to be forgiven.

But that's not how **this** story ends.

Chapter 28

Mini-feature: "Internet Legends of East Asia: Reddit, LINE, and YouTube"

"They say don't click strange links. Don't open that chat. Don't watch the whole video. Why? Because not all ghosts are analog anymore."

You get a message from an unknown number.

Just a link.

No context. No name.

You click.

The video is only a few seconds long.

A face. Too close. Not blinking.

Then your screen goes black.

Then your **lights**.

And somewhere on your phone, your **front camera turns on.**

Welcome to modern haunting.

This isn't a graveyard story.

This is horror in **real time.**

LINE and the Ghost in the Chat

In **Japan** and **Korea**, LINE is the most popular messaging app.

And it's also home to **ghost stories in real time.**

These stories often follow a familiar formula:

- You get a LINE message from a dead friend
- They ask for help. Or just say "hello."
- You block them… and they make a new account
- Their photo changes. Their tone shifts.
- They send you a picture of **your house.**
- Then… **they stop typing.**

And that's when the **real knock** comes.

YouTube Horror: Livestreams You Shouldn't Finish

East Asian horror creators have taken to YouTube with **deeply immersive, found-footage nightmares.**

Common tropes:

- Livestream ghost hunts where **the streamer disappears mid-broadcast**

- Viewers warned: "Don't keep watching if the screen turns red"

- Comment sections full of users saying, *"My lights flickered during this."*

- Hauntings that evolve **after watching** the video—blamed on cursed audio or hidden symbols

Some say you only get haunted if you **watch the whole thing.**

Others say just seeing the **thumbnail** is enough.

Reddit and the Dark Ritual Threads

Sites like Reddit (especially r/NoSleep, r/ThreeKings, and r/LetsNotMeet) are rich with **ritual horror games** that trace their roots to East Asian legends.

Popular "games" include:

- **The Elevator Game**

- **Daruma-san** (a Japanese ghost in the bathtub who chases you all day)

- **Hide-and-Seek Alone** (*Hitori Kakurenbo*) with a stuffed doll and salt water

- **The Red Room Curse**: a pop-up that asks "Do you like the Red Room?" If you can't close it, you're already dead

Each has specific rules.

All end the same:

If you mess up—even once—**you're not alone anymore.**

Horror That's Watching You

Themes found in modern East Asian internet horror:

- Ghosts that **learn**

- AI that turns on you

- Livestreams that keep going after the host is gone

- Comments that appear **after you post**, from **you**, but you didn't write them

- Video filters revealing **figures that aren't visible in the room**

Because in these stories, it's not about the curse.

It's about **you becoming part of it.**

Why These Stories Work

Internet horror in East Asia blends:

- Ancient beliefs in **spirits, rules,** and **rituals**

- Modern fears about **privacy, surveillance,** and **isolation**

- A cultural thread that says: if something goes wrong, it might not be **random**

It's not just fear. It's **control** slipping.

And you don't need a haunted house.

Just a bad connection.

- **Scare Rating:** 💀 💀 💀 💀
- **Sources:** Reddit, LINE, TikTok, YouTube, Korean message boards
- **Top Stories:** The Red Room Curse, The Whisper Game, Daruma-san, ghost livestreams
- **Recurring Elements:** Glitches, surveillance, haunted AI, "don't watch this" warnings
- **Survival Tips:** Don't click unknown links. Don't watch cursed videos alone. Don't say yes to a message you didn't ask for.

Final Words

The screen is just a screen.

Until it isn't.

A message arrives.

You don't remember signing up for anything.

It says one word:

Hello.

And now the typing bubble's blinking.

E.V. Nocturne

And your webcam light just flicked on.

Not all ghosts need to knock.

Some just need **signal**.

Part 6

Oceania – Lights, Beasts, and Ancient Terrors

Here, the ground remembers. The sky watches. And the silence carries more than just the wind. In the ancient spaces of Australia and Aotearoa, legends don't die. They just shift shape —and wait.

Chapter 29
Min Min Lights (Australia)

"They drift out of the desert like ghosts made of fire. You can run. You can turn around. But they'll still be there—just behind you, flickering."

You're driving through the Outback, and it's well past midnight.

No towns. No lights. Just red earth, gum trees, and sky.

Your high beams carve a narrow path through the dark.

And then, just over the next rise—

You see it.

A light. Floating above the road.

It's not from a car.

It's too low for a plane.

Too bright to be a reflection.

And it's **moving toward you**.

You slow down. It doesn't stop.

Welcome to **Min Min country.**

And now that it's found you...

it won't let go.

The First Light Never Fades

The **Min Min Lights** are one of Australia's most enduring—and unnerving—mysteries.

They've been seen for generations:

- By **stockmen** riding alone
- By **truck drivers** crossing the desert
- By **campers** who never came back

Named after the now-abandoned **Min Min Hotel** near Boulia, Queensland, where one of the earliest modern sightings occurred in 1918.

A man saw a strange glowing orb rise from the graveyard behind the hotel, hover, and follow him for kilometers.

Since then, the lights have followed **many**.

And the stories always end the same way:

"It was right behind me... but when I turned around—it was farther away. Still watching."

. . .

What They Look Like

Descriptions vary—but a few details are always the same:

- Floating orbs of light, often **white, green, or orange**

- The size of a soccer ball or lantern

- Silent. **Always silent.**

- Appear on the horizon... then **close the distance without moving**

They don't blink.

They don't flicker like fire.

They hover.

They follow.

Sometimes for minutes.

Sometimes for **hours**.

And the worst part?

They mimic **headlights**—until you're too close to run.

The Rules of the Lights

If you see a Min Min light:

- **Don't chase it**

- **Don't stop**

- **Don't try to take photos** (they never come out)

- Most of all—**don't follow it**

Because some believe they **lure people into the desert**, where the land swallows them.

No wreckage. No bodies.

Just silence.

And sometimes, their own light joins the rest.

Science Tries—and Fails

Explanations have been offered:

- **Fata Morgana** mirage effects
- **Bioluminescent gas** from decomposing plants
- Light refracted through heat and dust
- **Static electricity** or rare air plasma phenomena

But even scientists who study the lights admit:

"They don't behave like anything we understand."

Why do they move **against the wind**?

Why do they follow vehicles and walkers?

Why do they sometimes appear to **react** to being watched?

Some things the land just won't explain.

What Elders Say

For Aboriginal Australians, these lights aren't "new."

Stories of glowing spirits in the desert go back generations:

- **Restless souls** of those who died alone
- **Ancestral warnings** to keep off sacred land
- **Mischievous spirits** sent to test the living

In some regions, they're known as:

- *"Warruwi"* (in Arrernte tradition)
- Or simply **"death lights"**

And the message is simple:

"If it follows you, you're not supposed to be there."

Modern Encounters

You'll still hear the stories:

- A camper in Birdsville watches one follow him to the edge of his tent.
- A truck driver says the light hovered above his cab for hours—and the radio cut out.
- A hiker in the Northern Territory saw two lights circle him until sunrise.

Photos? Always blurry.

Videos? Batteries drain.

Proof? **Not really the point.**

Because in Min Min country, **you either believe the story—or become one.**

- **Truth Meter:** 🔦 Widely reported phenomenon with no scientific consensus
- **Regions:** Queensland, Northern Territory, parts of Western Australia
- **Tell-Tale Signs:** Silent orbs, no visible source, movement that defies logic
- **Best Advice:** Don't follow the lights. Don't test them. Don't think they're there *for you.*

Final Words

You drive faster.

The road's still straight. Still empty.

But the light is gone.

Or maybe it's just out of view.

Waiting at the next bend.

Hovering near the next signpost.

Warming up for the next story.

Because the Min Min Lights don't disappear.

They **choose someone else**.

And if the sky is clear enough tonight...

that someone might be **you.**

Chapter 30
Taniwha (New Zealand/Maori)

"Some protect. Some destroy. All remember. And when they rise, it's already too late to turn back."

You're walking near a river bend. The air is still.

Too still.

Birds stop singing. The current slows.

The ground hums beneath your feet—not loud, but **ancient**.

Then you feel it.

Like a thought in your spine.

Like something beneath the water has turned and **seen you.**

You weren't supposed to come here.

This is the domain of the **Taniwha**.

And now, **you're standing on its back.**

What Is a Taniwha?

To outsiders, it might sound like a mythological monster.

But in **Māori tradition**, the **Taniwha** is far more than that.

It is:

- A **guardian**

- A **beast**

- A **kaitiaki**—a protector of sacred places and people

- Or, depending on how it's treated, a **destroyer**

Taniwha often live in:

- **Rivers, caves, lakes, or the sea**

- Deep underground or inside sacred mountains

- Places where the natural world feels… *heavier*

They are **older than humans.**

And they **choose who lives and who disappears.**

What They Look Like

Their forms shift from iwi to iwi (tribe to tribe), but common descriptions include:

- Massive **serpents**, often resembling giant eels or dragons

- Creatures with **gills and claws**, glowing eyes, and spined tails

- Sometimes appearing as **sharks, whales, or lizards**
- Others take **human form**—but never for long

Some are seen glowing beneath the waves.

Some are only ever felt—by the sound of water moving without reason.

And some are heard breathing in caves that no one dares to enter.

Guardians and Punishers

Taniwha aren't mindless.

They are **deeply moral**, governed by tapu (sacred law) and whakapapa (ancestral lineage).

They might:

- **Protect** a tribe, marae (meeting ground), or sacred spring
- **Warn** communities of impending danger—like earthquakes or floods
- **Punish** disrespect, desecration, or **unauthorized trespass**
- **Claim** lives of those who ignore signs or break tapu

If a road is planned through a sacred cave—**Taniwha protest.**

If someone drowns in calm water—**Taniwha justice.**

And locals know not to ask **why.**

Only **what was broken.**

. . .

Real Stories from Aotearoa

The Taniwha aren't just legends.

They're **still believed**—and still respected.

- In the early 2000s, a **highway project near Waikato** was delayed and re-routed due to protests involving a **Taniwha-guarded cave**

- Elders have warned journalists and politicians against entering certain valleys without proper **karakia (prayers)**

- In 2010, Māori groups blamed a **spate of drownings** on the disturbance of a sacred river habitat near Northland

The message is always the same:

"You were warned."

What the Taniwha Means

The Taniwha is **not a monster**.

It is:

- A force of nature with a memory

- A guardian of **balance, sacredness, and land**

- A symbol of the **living connection** between people and place

- A reminder that **colonial boundaries mean nothing to ancient spirits**

It doesn't roar.

It doesn't chase.

It waits—**patient and sovereign**.

And when it rises, it doesn't ask questions.

Taniwha in Pop Culture

While rarely commercialized, the Taniwha appears in:

- **Local films** (e.g. *Mataku*, *Taniwha*, *The Dead Lands*)
- **Māori TV storytelling** and oral histories
- **Educational programs** that frame it as both a legend and a **cultural landmark**
- **Legal battles** over land, where ancestral sites tied to Taniwha are protected

It is one of the rare spirits still **recognized in law, land, and lore.**

- **Scare Rating:** 💀 💀 💀 💀
- **Truth Meter:** Deep traditional belief, still culturally and politically active
- **Habitat:** Waterways, caves, deep forest, sacred earth
- **Forms:** Serpent, shark, eel, dragon, shapeshifter
- **Key Traits:** Territorial, ancestral, bound by sacred law (tapu)

Final Words

The wind picks up.

The water stirs.

You think it's coincidence.

But the birds don't return.

The river no longer flows as it did.

And your guide won't look you in the eye.

"We shouldn't be here," they whisper.

And you realize the story was never fiction.

The Taniwha was here **before you**.

And now, it knows your name.

Chapter 31
The Dreamtime Beings (Aboriginal Australia)

"Before rivers flowed. Before stars blinked. Before even memory—They moved. And where they moved, the world became."

You feel it before you hear it.

A hum, deep underfoot.

Not sound exactly—**something older.**

The wind stills. The earth doesn't.

And for a moment, the land itself feels awake.

This is not a story.

This is not a myth.

This is **Dreaming country**.

And the Beings are watching.

. . .

What Is the Dreaming?

To Western minds, it's often misnamed as "myth" or "legend."

But in **Aboriginal cultures**, the **Dreaming** (or *Tjukurpa, Alcheringa, Ngarrangkarni,* etc.) is a **sacred, living truth**.

It refers to:

• The **time before time**, when **Ancestral Beings** created the land, animals, sky, and laws

• The **beings themselves**, who still exist—beneath the surface, in the rock, water, and sky

• A **spiritual map** that connects people to place, to ancestors, to all of creation

Dreamtime isn't in the past.

It's **always now.**

Who the Beings Are

There are thousands of stories, differing between language groups and nations—but a few figures are universally powerful:

The Rainbow Serpent (*Ngalyod, Wagyl,* etc.)

• Carved rivers and valleys with its coils

• Both **creator and destroyer**

• Associated with rain, fertility, and punishment

• Angered when waterholes or sacred sites are disturbed

Bunjil (Eaglehawk) – Wurundjeri

- Creator of the mountains, rivers, and the laws
- Watches from the sky, judging human behavior

Wandjina – Kimberley region

- Rain and cloud spirits painted in caves
- Depicted with **no mouths**—because their power is spoken through weather, not words
- Their images are sacred and **must not be altered**

Daramulum – Eora

- Sky spirit, son of Baiame
- Walks between worlds, especially at **night**, and is sometimes blamed for **strange lights or dreams**

These are not "characters."

These are **law-beings**, living forces woven into **land, spirit, and identity.**

What Happens If You Disturb Them

Dreamtime beings **can still be angered**.

- Mining sites desecrating sacred rock art
- Waterholes drained
- Tourists climbing places they were told not to
- Artifacts removed without permission

When this happens, stories tell of:

- **Sudden storms**
- **Spates of death or sickness**
- Travelers **getting lost** in the bush—even on marked trails
- Dreams where the being appears, **angry, warning, waiting**

Some say the land shifts underfoot.

That animals vanish.

That time bends.

That the Being has returned.

How They're Seen

- In **cave paintings** tens of thousands of years old
- In **songlines**—pathways across the land that encode sacred geography
- In **bodies of water, trees, and mountains**, each representing part of a being's story
- In **ritual, dance**, and **ceremony**—when Dreamtime becomes now again

What the Dreamtime Means

The Dreamtime is not fantasy.

It is:

- A **spiritual topography**—a map where story, land, and soul are one

- A **living moral code**—what's sacred, what's taboo, what's human

- A deep-rooted expression of **identity, survival, and law**

You don't "believe" in Dreamtime Beings.

You **walk where they walked.**

You **sleep on their backs.**

You **breathe what they left behind.**

Tourist Warnings That Go Ignored

Places connected to Dreamtime Beings often come with warnings:

- "Do not take rocks from this land"

- "Do not swim in this waterhole"

- "Do not speak their name aloud here"

Yet every year, visitors break the rules.

And every year, stories circulate of:

- **Car crashes after taking a stone from Uluru**

- **Equipment malfunctions on sacred land**

- People reporting **nightmares, sickness, hallucinations** after visiting the wrong site without permission

Some return what they took—**by mail.**

Others... don't get the chance.

- **Scare Rating:** 💀💀💀💀💀 (especially when disrespect is involved)
- **Truth Meter:** 🪵 Not "ghost stories"—these are sacred cosmologies
- **Key Beings:** Rainbow Serpent, Bunjil, Wandjina, Daramulum
- **How They Appear:** Through dreams, storms, cave art, lost paths, natural formations
- **Rules:** Don't disturb sacred sites. Don't mimic sacred art. Don't treat these stories as fiction.

Final Words

You thought it was just a hill.

Just a trail. Just a rock.

But now you can't sleep.

Your compass spins. Your camera won't work.

The locals won't meet your eye.

And at night, you hear something—not a voice, not an animal.

Something deeper. **Older.**

You walked through their memory.

Now, **they're in yours.**

And they do not forget.

Chapter 32
The Night Parrot Curse (Outback legend)

"They say if you find it, something else finds you. And after that... things start to go wrong."

You see a blur of green in the torchlight.

A flash of feathers, a rustle in the grass.

You lift your binoculars.

Your heart skips—you know what it is.

A **Night Parrot.**

So rare it's called a **ghost bird**.

So elusive some still believe it's a **spirit, not a species.**

You smile.

But something in the back of your mind twists.

Because everyone who's found it...

Starts to lose something else.

The Ghost Bird

The **Night Parrot (Pezoporus occidentalis)** is a real animal—one of the rarest, most secretive birds on Earth.

- Native to remote Australian desert scrublands
- Thought extinct for over a century
- Rediscovered in 2013 after only a few contested sightings

Nocturnal. Nearly silent.

It lives in the middle of **nowhere**, and even then—only if it wants to be seen.

And some say... it **never wanted to be found.**

The Curse Begins

Ever since the rediscovery, strange patterns have emerged:

- Researchers who locate the bird suffer **sudden accidents**, **mental breakdowns**, or **disappear into isolation**
- Equipment fails
- Footage vanishes
- Locations become **untraceable**

Some say it's coincidence.

Others say it's guilt.

But in birding forums and hushed conservation circles, one phrase keeps coming back:

"Don't chase the Night Parrot too hard."

Because it **chases back.**

The Stories Behind the Silence

Before modern science got involved, the Night Parrot already had a legend among Outback locals and Aboriginal communities.

Some say:

- It's a **messenger spirit**, appearing before misfortune
- It is **guarded by Dreamtime protectors**, angered when disturbed
- It exists **between worlds**, and by finding it, you **open something**

Even some **scientists and park rangers** quietly admit they've felt strange energy in Night Parrot zones:

- Sudden disorientation
- Feeling watched
- Shadows that shouldn't be there
- Tech cutting out only when the bird appears

Why It's Feared by Those Who Should Know Better

One conservationist said:

"It's not that the parrot is dangerous. It's that what surrounds it is."

They don't just mean the harsh terrain.

They mean:

- Sacred land being disturbed in the name of science

- Greedy developers using the bird as leverage—then disappearing from the news

- Private trackers refusing to share coordinates, saying **"it's safer that way."**

And the few who've filmed it?

They speak less now.

Or not at all.

What the Bird Symbolizes

In folklore terms, the Night Parrot is a perfect storm of archetypes:

- **The sacred creature** that disappears when the world stops deserving it

- **The forbidden knowledge** that punishes those who seek it without respect

- **A living riddle**—and like all riddles, dangerous if solved incorrectly

It is the fear of reaching **too far**, of thinking **everything must be seen**.

Some things exist to **be heard once and never again.**

Modern Appearances (and Vanishings)

- **Photos** exist, but are rare and often contested
- **Field recordings** capture faint calls—but are sometimes lost in crashes
- **Expeditions** are highly controlled, with GPS data often encrypted or hidden

Even in 2020s documentaries, the Night Parrot is often mentioned more as **legend** than specimen.

Because science may have confirmed it…

But the **bush**?

The **bush still hides it.**

And the bush keeps score.

- **Scare Rating:** 💀 💀 💀 💀
- **Truth Meter:** A real bird surrounded by very real fear
- **Known Habitat:** Queensland, Western Australia—exact locations are protected
- **How to Find It:** You don't. It finds you.
- **Field Tips:** If you hear a short, metallic "ding"—turn around. Or don't.

Final Words

You mark the coordinates.

You take the photo.

You're smiling. You did it. You're in the books now.

But back in camp, the wind doesn't feel right.

The shadows move when they shouldn't.

And the desert no longer feels quiet.

They say you shouldn't chase ghosts.

And you definitely shouldn't catch them.

Because now you've seen the Night Parrot…

What's going to see you?

Chapter 33

Mini-feature: "The Outback: A Natural Setting for Fear"

"It's not haunted houses that scare people here. It's the space. The silence. The knowing that no one is coming if something goes wrong."

The Outback doesn't need monsters.

It doesn't creak like old floorboards.

It doesn't flicker like candlelight.

It **doesn't move**—but it feels like it watches.

The terror here isn't always supernatural.

It's **elemental**.

The sun burns. The wind whispers. The land swallows without effort.

And when fear does arrive, it doesn't knock.

It just **waits**.

Space That Watches

In Australia's interior, the distances aren't just vast—they're **unnatural**.

You drive for hours without seeing another soul.

No signs. No fences.

Just red soil and blue sky until both blur.

It plays tricks on you:

- **Mirages** shimmer like lakes

- **Shadows** seem to move when they shouldn't

- The landscape starts to feel **too quiet**, like it's holding its breath

Even seasoned travelers speak of the **Outback stare**—a hollow-eyed silence that comes from being **alone too long**.

Why the Outback Breeds Myth

Legends cling to this land because:

- **Voices carry farther than footsteps**

- You can scream, and no one will hear

- **Sacred places** remain undisturbed for millennia

- The **boundaries between life, memory, and spirit** are thin out here

Stories like:

- The **Min Min Lights**, flickering just ahead
- The **Night Parrot**, found only when it wants to be
- The **Rainbow Serpent**, coiled beneath dried rivers
- Lost explorers who vanish with no trace—except for maybe a boot, or a torn tent flap

These stories survive not just because they're spooky...

But because they feel **true** the moment you're out there.

What the Fear Feels Like

It's not a jump scare.

It's slower. Heavier.

The kind that grows from:

- **No reception**
- A map that doesn't match the road
- Footprints that appear beside yours in sand where no one else should be
- The feeling of being **watched in a place with no eyes**

Nature as Ghost Story

The Outback doesn't need spirits to haunt you.

The land itself can:

- Take your vehicle
- Twist your compass
- Hide your tracks
- **Whisper through wind and ruin**

And when you try to explain it later, it sounds like madness:

"I saw something. I heard... something."

"I don't know why I turned around—but I had to."

Sometimes, that's the Outback talking.

And sometimes... it's something **older**.

- **Scare Rating:** 💀 💀 💀 💀 💀 (if you're alone long enough)
- **Fear Type:** Psychological, environmental, ancestral
- **Legends Born Here:** Min Min Lights, Bunyip, Night Parrot, Lost Explorers
- **Common Themes:** Isolation, elemental punishment, sacred land retribution
- **Modern Survival Tip:** Bring water. Tell someone where you're going. And **listen when locals say not to camp there.**

Final Words

The Outback doesn't whisper.

It waits.

And in its silence, you'll hear things—footsteps behind you, echoes without source, voices in the wind.

Maybe it's the heat.

Maybe it's the emptiness.

Or maybe this place has a memory.

And it remembers **every footstep**, every trespass, every story buried under dust.

Because in the Outback, **you're not just walking through land**—

You're walking through **legend**.

And sometimes... **it walks back.**

CONCLUSION
Why We Keep Believing

"There's a knock at the door. You're alone. It's after midnight. You already know what this book would tell you to do. Don't answer."

We tell ourselves these are just stories.

Words passed around the fire, between locker doors, through forum threads and message apps at 2 a.m.

We laugh.

We shiver.

We say we don't believe.

But we still turn on the lights when we walk past the mirror.

We still avoid the forest trail after dark.

We still hesitate—just for a second—when someone knocks unexpectedly.

CONCLUSION

Why?

Because the legends we've told across this book—Bloody Mary, the Taniwha, La Llorona, the Night Whistler—they **aren't real**... not exactly.

They're something worse.

They're **almost real.**

Fear as Memory, Dressed as Story

Urban legends are not just entertainment.

They are **emotional fossils**—pressure-formed truths hardened into warnings.

- Slender Man wasn't born evil. He was born of **internet chaos and loneliness**.

- Pinky Pinky wasn't a monster—she was a mirror of **post-apartheid fear and gender violence**.

- The Dreamtime Beings? They are still here. Still sacred. Still shaping the land.

These stories wear different masks in different cultures, but they all ask the same question:

Are you sure you're safe?

The Psychology of a Shiver

We are wired to seek patterns, to fear what lurks outside the light.

Our ancestors survived by flinching at rustling leaves and shadows that moved wrong.

CONCLUSION

Modern life dulled the edges, but **our brains remember**:

- That feeling when the hair on your arms stands up
- When you know someone's watching—but no one's there
- When you hear your name whispered, and no one called

Urban legends are the **training grounds** for fear:

- They let us rehearse danger
- They give form to anxiety
- They offer rules—simple, elegant, terrifying

"Don't whistle at night."

"Don't say her name in the mirror."

"Don't get off the elevator if she gets on."

We memorize these not because we believe them…

but because **what if**?

Legends That Evolve

The monsters of folklore never die.

They just migrate.

- The jinn move from desert to Discord
- The Woman in White updates her wardrobe, but keeps her scream
- The elevator game now plays out in TikTok challenges

We stream our hauntings.

CONCLUSION

We tag our curses.

We film our ghosts in 4K.

But the rules haven't changed.

We still summon.

We still suffer.

We still warn the next person: *"Don't do what I did."*

Responsibility in the Retelling

Not all stories belong to everyone.

Some were shaped through sacred ceremony.

Some are still part of active religious or cultural practice.

Some carry the weight of colonization, silence, and loss.

It matters **how** we tell them.

It matters **why** we tell them.

The difference between folklore and exploitation is **respect**.

Fear is powerful.

But so is **memory**.

And for many of these tales, memory is sacred.

The Real Reason We Keep the Stories Alive

We believe not because we're gullible.

We believe because we're **human**.

CONCLUSION

Because some part of us remembers:

- The forest doesn't always give back what it takes
- The ocean keeps secrets
- The night is not empty
- And names—names have power

We tell the stories because **we were told them once**, and it left a mark.

Now it's our turn.

And as long as someone's listening, the legend lives on.

Final Words

So here we are.

Book in your hands. Lights maybe still on. Shadows maybe still quiet.

But tomorrow, someone will say something odd:

"Don't go in that room after midnight."

"Hold your breath when you drive past that house."

"If you hear a knock late at night—don't open it."

And you'll remember this.

Not as proof. Not as belief.

But as a whisper.

Because fear doesn't care if you believe.

CONCLUSION

It only cares that you **heard**.

And now you have.

THE END

(unless something knocks.)

Appendix

The story's over. But if you're still reading... maybe you're not done yet..

Appendix

Here you'll find a toolkit for digging deeper: words to know, stories to chase, creators to follow, and rabbit holes that might keep you up at night. You've been warned.

Glossary of Horror & Folklore Terms

- **Creepypasta** – Internet-born horror stories shared across forums, often evolving over time; digital folklore for the age of Wi-Fi.

- **Legend** – A traditional story often rooted in history or belief, but exaggerated or unverifiable.

- **Myth** – A sacred or foundational story explaining the origins of a culture, people, or place.

- **Folklore** – The collective stories, traditions, and superstitions passed through a community over generations.

- **Urban Legend** – A modern myth told as true, often shared via word-of-mouth, chain emails, forums, or group chats.

- **Tulpa** – A concept from Tibetan mysticism, now popular in paranormal lore; a thought-form that becomes real through belief.

- **Tropes** – Recurring themes or storytelling devices in horror (e.g., "the final girl," "the haunted mirror," "don't look back").

- **Kaitiaki** – In Māori belief, a guardian spirit, often tied to the land or a specific place or family line.

- **Tapu** – A concept of sacred restriction in Māori culture—places, people, or actions considered spiritually off-limits.

- **The Dreaming** – In Aboriginal Australian cultures, the

timeless "before-time" where ancestral spirits shaped the land and still reside.

Further Reading & Resources

If this book kept you turning pages after midnight, here's more for your haunted library:

Books

• *The Vanishing Hitchhiker* by Jan Harold Brunvand — Classic collection of American urban legends.

• *Kwaidan: Stories and Studies of Strange Things* by Lafcadio Hearn — Japanese ghost stories and folklore.

• *Monsters of the Week* by Zachary Ingle & David Sutera — Exploring modern myths through media and pop culture.

• *Cursed Objects* by J.W. Ocker — A tour of real-life haunted and taboo artifacts around the world.

Folklore Archives

• The Folklore Society (UK)

• American Folklife Center – Library of Congress

• AustLit: Aboriginal & Torres Strait Islander Stories

Creator / Source Credits (Especially for Internet-Born Myths)

Urban legends don't come from nowhere—many are the product of brilliant, anonymous, or often overlooked storytellers. Where possible, we've credited original creators:

- **Slender Man** – Created by *Eric Knudsen (aka Victor Surge)* on the Something Awful forums, 2009.

- **The Rake** – Spread through 4chan's /x/ board and creepypasta.com; earliest documentation: 2006 blog posts.

- **The Elevator Game** – First appeared on Korean forums around 2010; translated versions spread through Reddit and creepypasta fandoms.

- **Daruma-san** (Japanese ritual ghost) – Origin unclear; popularized via chain emails, Reddit threads, and YouTube in the early 2010s.

- **Red Room Curse** – Based on a Japanese internet pop-up legend that allegedly inspired crimes; source roots back to early 2000s flash sites.

If you're telling these stories—respect the originators. These myths are collaborative, evolving, and deeply human.

TikTok / YouTube Channels & Podcasts to Explore

The modern campfire is a ring light or a mic. These creators keep the legends alive—one scream at a time.

TikTok / YouTube Horror Creators

- **@theghostinmymachine** – Bite-sized haunted objects, rituals, and urban myths.

- **@hauntedsandwich** – Folklore deep dives with creepy edits and historical context.

- **@brandonjmcdermott** – Spooky storytelling meets historical horror.

Appendix

- **Nexpo (YouTube)** – Internet mysteries and dark web legends, beautifully produced.

- **Wendigoon (YouTube)** – Longform, friendly deep dives into obscure horror lore, ARGs, and creepypastas.

- **Night Mind (YouTube)** – Analysis of ARGs and online horror fiction like *Marble Hornets*.

Podcasts

- **Lore** – Haunting historical horror, narrated by Aaron Mahnke.

- **The Magnus Archives** – Fictional horror anthology, cult classic status.

- **Let's Not Meet** – Real stories of true creepy encounters.

- **Unwell** – Midwestern gothic audio drama with folklore themes.

- **Scare You To Sleep** – Horror stories read softly, to unsettling effect.

Final Note

Every generation finds new ways to share old fears.

Whether it's a whispered ghost story or a viral TikTok about a haunted hallway, what matters is that the legend **lives on**— and we pass it on with care, curiosity, and just enough fear to **make it real** again.

www.ingramcontent.com/pod-product-compliance
Lightning Source LLC
LaVergne TN
LVHW011932070526
838202LV00054B/4607